101 Questions and Answers on Paul

101 QUESTIONS AND ANSWERS ON PAUL

Ronald D. Witherup, S.S.

PAULIST PRESS
New York/Mahwah, N.J.

In memory of Raymond E. Brown, S.S.
1928–1998

Nihil Obstat: Reverend Frank J. Matera, Ph.D.,
The Catholic University of America
Imprimatur: Most Reverend W. Francis Malooly, V.G.,
Archdiocese of Baltimore

Book design by Theresa M. Sparacio

Cover design by Cynthia Dunne

Library of Congress Cataloging-in-Publication Data

Witherup, Ronald D., 1950–
    101 questions and answers on Paul / Ronald D. Witherup.
        p. cm.
    Includes bibliographical references.
    ISBN 0-8091-4180-9 (alk. paper)
    1. Paul, the Apostle, Saint—Miscellanea. I. Title: One hundred and one questions and answers on Paul. II. Title: One hundred one questions and answers on Paul. III. Title.
BS2506.3 .W58 2003
225.9′2—dc21

                                                    2003004563

Published by Paulist Press
997 Macarthur Boulevard
Mahwah, New Jersey 07430

www.paulistpress.com

Printed and bound in the
United States of America

CONTENTS

LIST OF ABBREVIATIONS

AB   Anchor Bible

NAB   The New American Bible with Revised New Testament and Revised Psalms (1987)

NRSV New Revised Standard Version

NT   New Testament

OT   Old Testament

RSV   Revised Standard Version (Second Edition, 1971)

PREFACE

This series was begun quite incidentally by Raymond E. Brown's bestseller, *Responses to 101 Questions on the Bible* (1990). His book spontaneously struck a chord that encouraged others to write in the same genre to which the present book aspires. Originally I had intended to dedicate this book to Father Brown in 1998 on the occasion of his 70th birthday and 45th anniversary of ordination to the priesthood. Sadly, that is the year he died, on August 8, 1998, before I could finish the manuscript and before he could know my intentions to honor him. Various other pressing duties subsequently prevented me from getting back to the manuscript that I now dedicate to his memory. Paradoxically, this book will appear on the occasion of what would have been Father Brown's 75th birthday and 50th anniversary of ordination. An internationally acclaimed biblical scholar who was widely respected for his judicious and comprehensive approach to biblical studies, Father Brown also had a gift for communicating the fruits of modern biblical scholarship to average clergy or lay people in a nontechnical fashion. In doing so, he led many people to encounter the Word of God more intimately than they could have dreamed. I can only hope that the present book will, in its own small way, imitate and pay homage to his refined style.

I wish to thank Father Lawrence Boadt, publisher of Paulist Press, for his extreme patience and helpful guidance on this project, and the staff of Paulist Press for their fine oversight of the book's production. My gratitude also extends to friends and colleagues, especially to Professors Frank J. Matera, Michael J. Gorman, and Thomas R. Hurst, S.S., for their many insightful comments and recommendations. Additionally, I thank Reverend Jason A. Glover who efficiently accomplished the tedious task of checking the biblical quotations and references and who made many suggestions regarding style. While I remain fully responsible for the text, I have benefited greatly from their sharp eyes and even sharper intellect.

R. D. W.

Solemnity of Peter and Paul, 2002

INTRODUCTION

This book grew out of the experience of teaching the letters of Paul to seminarians, priests and ministers, and lay adult education groups. Questions always arose that people wished to have addressed, and I found their questions both stimulating and challenging. I had to seek ways to explain some rather abstract concepts, such as Paul's theological views, in a manner that was understandable yet true to Paul's writings. Like many Christians I have found Paul sometimes difficult to understand. Paul's letters often produce more questions than answers. In the course of writing this book, I almost thought 1001 questions would have been a better format. More questions remain than I have been able to address, and I am left with the same feeling with which I began: Of all the great figures of Christian antiquity that I would like to have a conversation with, Paul would be the first. Unfortunately, in his personal absence, he has left only letters, and these will have to suffice for the task at hand.

I had qualms about this task from another perspective. It seemed like such an act of pride to attempt to address questions about Paul and his letters that scholars have debated through the ages without reaching definitive conclusions. Despite the brevity of some of his letters, they are often filled with passages that are either obscure or that seem to fly in the face of contemporary tendencies. We can take some comfort in knowing that Paul's letters sparked controversy since the earliest days of Christianity. The author of Second Peter, probably the last NT writing, warns his readers:

Therefore, beloved, while you are waiting for these
things, strive to be found by him at peace, without spot
or blemish; and regard the patience of our Lord as salvation. So also our beloved brother Paul wrote to you
according to the wisdom given him, speaking of this as
he does in all his letters. There are some things in them
hard to understand, which the ignorant and unstable
twist to their own destruction, as they do the other
scriptures. (2 Pet 3:14–16)

Paul's concepts are sometimes quite easy to misread. Unlike Second Peter, I do not believe the "ignorant and unstable" are the only
ones capable of misusing or misunderstanding Paul's writings.

I write this book with the conviction that many people have
often misunderstood Paul. I think he has been blamed wrongly for
intolerant attitudes, especially with regard to some of his ethical
teachings. Some of this confusion is due to taking his writings out
of context. We forget that his letters were "occasional," that is,
composed with specific occasions and audiences in mind. He
wrote them to particular congregations at particular times and
under particular circumstances. Yet because his letters are so
prominent in the NT and in Christian history, their influence has
extended far beyond the Christian communities he evangelized in
the first century. Paul's letters in every age have evoked positive
and negative assessments. You either like him or you don't. He is
not a figure that induces indifference.

Most exemplary of the negative views of Paul is the judgment
that he distorted Jesus' teaching. Some have deemed Paul the
"founder of Christianity." They think that he is the one who organized the Christian religion. He went far beyond what Jesus
intended and in doing so distorted the gospel message. This attitude
spans centuries. In the nineteenth century Friedrich Nietzsche, the
German philosopher, could write:

The "glad tidings" were followed closely by the absolutely worst tidings—those of St. Paul. Paul is the incarnation of a type which is the reverse of that of the Saviour; he is the genius in hatred....And alas what did this dysangelist not sacrifice to his hatred! Above all the Saviour himself: he nailed him to his cross. Christ's life, his example, his doctrine and death, the sense and the right of the gospel—not a vestige of all this was left, once this forger, prompted by his hatred, had understood in it only that which could serve his purpose....The type of the Saviour, his teaching, his life, his death, even the sequel to his death—nothing remained untouched, nothing was left which even remotely resembled reality. St. Paul simply transferred the centre of gravity of the whole of that great life, to a place behind this life,—in the lie of the "resuscitated" Christ. (In "The Jewish Dysangelist" [1888], quoted in Wayne Meeks [ed.], *The Writings of St. Paul* [New York: W. W. Norton, 1972], pp. 294–95. [Note Nietzsche's invention of the word "dysangelist" as a kind of anti-evangelist.])

We might at first be tempted to dismiss this assessment by a notoriously mean-spirited critic of religion from a bygone era. Then we realize that such a negative view of Paul is alive and well in our own day. Stephen Mitchell, who authored a recent book on Jesus, views Paul as "the most misleading of the earliest Christian writers...in a spiritual sense, he was very unripe" (*The Gospel According to Jesus* [San Francisco: Harper, 1992], p. 41). Moreover, the popular British historian A. N. Wilson has written a book that resurrects the idea that Paul is the one who first misdirected Christianity (*Paul: The Mind of the Apostle* [New York: W. W. Norton, 1998]).

Paul, however, also has a fan club. As early as the heretic Marcion (ca. A.D. 85–160), there were those who saw Paul as one who embodied the authentic Christian attitudes that contrasted strongly with those of the OT. Marcion included ten of Paul's letters in his highly selective canon of sacred writings. The Church quickly found Marcion's judgments to be too narrow, especially with regard to cutting out the OT entirely. But he gave impetus to the collection of Paul's letters. A little later, John Chrysostom, a fourth-century theologian and Archbishop of Constantinople, extolled Paul in this fashion:

> As I keep hearing the Epistles of blessed Paul read, and that twice every week, and often three or four times, whenever we are celebrating the memorials of the holy martyrs, gladly do I enjoy the spiritual trumpet, and get roused and warmed with desire at recognizing the voice so dear to me, and seem to fancy him all but present to my sight, and behold him conversing with me. But I grieve and am pained, that all people do not know this man, as much as they ought to know him; but some are so far ignorant of him, as not even to know for certainty the number of his Epistles. ("Homilies on the Epistle to the Romans," in *Nicene and Post-Nicene Fathers,* vol. 11, p. 335, taken from *The AGES Digital Library Collections,* Version 2.0 [Albany, Ore.: AGES Software, 1997])

An even more influential theologian, Martin Luther, writing centuries later used more exalted tones to praise a passage from Paul's Letter to the Romans:

> Then I began to understand that the justice of God is that by which the just lives by a gift of God, namely by faith. This, then, is the meaning: the justice of God is revealed by the gospel, viz. the passive justice with which merciful God justifies us by faith, as it is written, "The just one lives by faith." Here I felt that I was

altogether born again and had entered paradise itself through open gates. ("Preface to Latin Writings," quoted in Joseph A. Fitzmyer, *Romans* [AB 33; New York: Doubleday, 1993], p. 261)

Luther would, of course, go on to put these words into action in the formulation of the Lutheran faith. For many Protestants, Paul and his message are essential to Christian faith. But Paul looms so large in the NT that no one can afford to disregard him. Hate him or love him, you cannot ignore him.

This brings me to the purpose of this book. Books about Paul and his writings abound. This book is not a replacement for basic introductions to the Pauline letters. Even less is it a commentary on the many passages of Paul that address rather complex theological and pastoral questions. In keeping with the style of this 101 Questions and Answers series, the purpose is to collect, in a convenient format, responses to a broad array of questions about Paul. Some seventy percent of these questions have arisen spontaneously in the midst of lectures and discussions. Others flow directly from such questions that arise time and again when I discuss St. Paul with average Christians in the pews. Many questions clearly come from contemporary concerns about Christian morality. I have, for the sake of convenience, grouped questions according to seven main topical areas. Some of the questions I have received were given to me by students whom I invited at the beginning of courses on the Pauline writings to indicate what they wanted to learn. In some cases I have rewritten questions to have them address the broadest issue possible, but I have striven to retain the flavor of the originals.

How should one use this book? I hope that it provides a good supplement to basic introductions to Paul for classroom or personal use. Readers can peruse the questions consecutively to obtain a broad overview of Paul in several areas. It can also be used to find a quick orientation to specific issues. The book moves from less complicated questions concerning Paul's life and background to much more complex ones dealing with theological and ethical issues. I note also that although I write from the perspective of a Roman Catholic, and periodically make reference to issues of interest to Catholics, the perspective of this book is nonetheless broadly ecumenical. Anyone interested in St. Paul can benefit from reflecting on these questions.

I add another word of advice. This book will be most helpful when used with a Bible at hand. I have endeavored as much as possible to use Paul's own words in response to questions. This means that I quote regularly from the NT or make frequent reference to passages that ought to be looked up, in order to get Paul's own perspective. This process may be a little more demanding, but it is more productive.

A danger exists in the format of a book like this. Readers may get the mistaken idea that it contains quick-fix answers to issues that are sometimes quite complex. As others who have written in this series have pointed out, these are responses rather than answers. Moreover, in the need to be selective, I am aware that I have left out many interesting and worthy questions. Nonetheless, within the limitations of such a format, I have tried to set the basic direction for reading Paul's letters in context. More thorough, yet popular, treatments can be found in the list of recommended readings that concludes this book. Although a question-response approach is no substitute for using commentaries on specific passages, it can provide a thumbnail sketch of this most fascinating of NT authors.

ONE

PAUL'S LIFE AND MINISTRY

1. We hear a lot of readings from St. Paul's letters at Sunday worship, but I find his writings hard to follow. Why do we read from his letters so often?

You are correct in your observation that Paul's letters appear often in the lectionary cycle. For Catholics and others who use a lectionary, Paul features prominently. You are also not alone in finding Paul difficult to understand. Many people find his writings to be rather abstract as compared with the Gospel stories. Yet there are reasons why we frequently hear Paul's letters in the Church's liturgy.

In the first place, many key ideas in Christianity originated with Paul, for example, Paul's understanding of justification by faith, the church as the body of Christ, or the three virtues—faith, hope, and love. Second, when the Catholic Church revised the order of the Mass after the Second Vatican Council and created the three-year lectionary cycle, one of the purposes of this new arrangement was to give Catholics greater exposure to the sacred scriptures. Prior to Vatican II, Catholics, in particular, had little formal exposure to Paul's letters. The breadth of the Bible can now be experienced at liturgy because of the new lectionary cycle. With thirteen of twenty-seven books of the NT bearing Paul's name, it is only natural to hear from him quite regularly.

A third reason concerns the structure of the lectionary. Paul's letters occur most often as the second reading at Sunday Mass. Sometimes the excerpt from Paul's writings may connect thematically with the other readings of the Mass, but more often they do not. These readings have themes that are usually independent of the other readings. You will notice that these excerpts from Paul's letters often continue for successive Sundays. This is called continuous or semicontinuous reading. This process allows Paul's letters to be read pretty much in their entirety, section by

section. This gives the impression that we are hearing a lot of
Paul. In reality this structure gives the opportunity to understand
Paul's writings in their own context, in which he addresses issue
after issue in the letters that he wrote.

Unfortunately, many preachers do not capitalize on this
revised structure. They seldom preach from these Pauline readings. This is a lost opportunity to help explain Paul and the major
features of his thought to their congregations. My hope is that this
book will provide an overview of Paul that will help people to
become more comfortable with Paul's letters.

2. How many letters did Paul write, and when were they written?

I will have more to say about Paul's letters in Part Four, but
it is useful to address this issue right away because it is so crucial
to many of the questions that follow. Your question would seemingly be easy to answer. All one would have to do is count the
number of letters that bear Paul's name in the table of contents of
a Bible. In reality, the question is more complicated.

The NT attributes thirteen letters to Paul. That is, they are
designated as "the Letter of Paul to such and such a community."
In canonical order the thirteen are: Romans, 1 and 2 Corinthians,
Galatians, Ephesians, Philippians, Colossians, 1 and 2 Thessalonians, 1 and 2 Timothy, Titus, and Philemon. Of these thirteen,
some scholars judge all of them to come from Paul himself or his
immediate followers. The majority of biblical scholars, however,
judges only seven of them to be from Paul himself. The seven
undisputed letters are: Romans, 1 and 2 Corinthians, Galatians,
Philippians, 1 Thessalonians, and Philemon. Of these, one should
note that several of them are "coauthored"; that is, some of Paul's
coworkers are listed along with Paul in the introduction and are
most likely to be considered authors as well (i.e., 1 and 2
Corinthians, Philippians, 1 Thessalonians, Philemon).

The remaining six letters are more controversial with respect
to authorship. Scholars are divided on the question of the origin of

all six of them. They are labeled the Deutero-Pauline letters, meaning "Second Paul." A common practice in the first century was to write documents in the name of a significant historical figure and attribute the document to that person. This practice may strike us as strange and illegitimate, but first-century people viewed authorship in a different fashion than we do. They were not bothered by the idea that someone might have written a document in someone else's name. This would be especially true of close colleagues or disciples. For one thing, it loaned authority to the message. Likewise it may have been an opportunity to write in the "spirit" of an earlier author but expand or develop that person's ideas.

In this book I take the majority opinion that the seven undisputed letters of Paul are the primary source for material on the authentic teaching of Paul. I also assume that the six other letters attributed to Paul are Deutero-Pauline written at a later time and from a later perspective. I believe, however, that they reflect genuinely Pauline ideas, consistent with or developing Paul's thought. Some scholars posit the existence of a "Pauline school" that could have been responsible for preserving and fostering Paul's letters. Some colleagues or disciples of Paul may have considered it their duty to preserve and evolve Paul's teachings.

One should not presume that everything in the Deutero-Pauline letters reflects non-Pauline thought. It is possible that individual passages in these latter six letters may be genuinely from the hand of Paul. One should also remember that many of the ideas expressed in these letters are consistent with Paul's own thought as developed in the undisputed letters. Some scholars take this latter notion as evidence that Paul's own ideas could have evolved in the course of time. They argue that the Deutero-Pauline letters could well be authentically Paul's own. For instance, some suggest that Second Timothy was written by Paul (or closer to his thought) and was used by others to compose First Timothy and Titus. This is always possible, and some good arguments have been presented to uphold this proposal. If one wanted to emphasize the probability of genuine Pauline authorship of the

Deutero-Pauline letters, we could chart this likelihood—from most likely to least likely—as follows: (1) 2 Thessalonians, (2) Colossians, (3) Ephesians, (4) 2 Timothy, (5) 1 Timothy/Titus. So far, however, I prefer to hold that these six letters stem from later hands, perhaps disciples of Paul. Yet I think they stand firmly in the Pauline tradition.

I conclude with a chart that shows the possible dates of the composition of Paul's letters in chronological order.

Letters	Approximate Date (A.D.)
1 Thessalonians	50–51
1 and 2 Corinthians	54–55
Galatians	54–55
Philippians	56
Romans	57–58
Philemon	60–61
2 Thessalonians	mid-80s (or 51–52 if genuine)
Colossians	mid-80s (or 54–56 if genuine)
Ephesians	mid-90s (or 60–63 if genuine)
2 Timothy	late 60s or mid- to late 90s (or 61–63 if genuine)
1 Timothy and Titus	late 60s or mid- to late 90s (or 62–64 if genuine)

3. Aren't the Gospels more important than Paul?

My response is both "yes" and "no." Yes, the four Gospels are more important than Paul in the sense that ancient tradition always venerated the Gospels in a special manner within the total NT tradition. This is understandable because the Gospels narrate the life of Jesus of Nazareth. Thus a hierarchy exists in the way Christians view the canon. Some books take precedent over others. In a similar fashion in the OT tradition, the first five books of the Bible, called the Torah (Hebrew) or the Pentateuch (Greek), were venerated in a special manner because they focused on the law.

Yet there is also a negative response your question. Christians view the entire Bible as canonical writing. This means that all parts of scripture are inspired by God and useful for Christian living. The word "canon" comes from the Greek word *kanōn,* which means a rule, a norm, or a measure. The notion that the entire Bible provides a yardstick by which Christians can measure their lives applies to all the books of the Bible. From this perspective we should consider Paul no less a source of the inspired Word of God than the Gospels themselves. A passage in Second Timothy conveys this sense: "All scripture is inspired by God and is useful for teaching, for reproof, for correction, and for training in righteousness, so that everyone who belongs to God may be proficient, equipped for every good work" (2 Tim 3:16–17). This does not mean that we will not find troublesome passages in the Bible that are either difficult to understand or appear hard to apply in our own day. However, it should remind us that the writings of Paul are no less a part of the scriptures than the Gospels.

4. What do we know about Paul's birth and upbringing?

The details of Paul's early life are rather sketchy. At the outset I emphasize the existence of a methodological problem: We have only two primary sources for the life of Paul, his own letters and the Acts of the Apostles. Sometimes these two sources are not in agreement. Generally, scholars take Paul's own testimony as the primary source for personal information about Paul. Acts functions as a supplementary and complementary source. Both sources must be used with caution when trying to deduce such historical information. Keeping this problem in mind, we can briefly summarize the main lines of Paul's early life.

Acts mentions that Paul was born in Tarsus, a large city in Cilicia, Asia Minor (Acts 9:11; 21:39; 22:3), in what is now Turkey. Paul never mentions Tarsus in his own letters. There is no reason to doubt that he was born in Tarsus. It was a Greco-Roman city with a sizable Jewish population. Paul would have been exposed to many aspects of both Jewish culture and Greco-Roman society. Acts does not explicitly tell us much about Paul's early life. An approximate date for his birth would be between A.D. 1 and 10. Nothing is known of his parents or his relatives. Acts 23:16 speaks of "the son of Paul's sister" (his nephew) who warns Paul of a plot to kill him; nothing else is known of other relatives. Paul's own letters add very little to this information. The last chapter of Romans refers by name to several "relatives" of Paul, Andronicus and Junia (Rom 16:7); Herodion (Rom 16:11); and Lucius, Jason, and Sosipater (Rom 16:21). These are not necessarily blood relatives. More likely Paul uses the word "relatives" in the sense of Romans 9:3 where he actually refers to fellow Jews. Acts mentions Sopater (shortened form of Sosipater) from Boerea as a companion of Paul when he fled from there (Acts 20:4). The name Jason also appears in Acts 17:5–9 as the host of Paul in Thessalonica, but it is uncertain whether he is the same person.

Paul does not write much about his pre-conversion life other than to indicate his Jewish Pharisaic background and his persecution of the church. In fact, he is eminently proud of his zeal as a Pharisee. The most prominent passage is Philippians 3:5–6 where Paul lists key elements of his background: "circumcised on the eighth day, a member of the people of Israel, of the tribe of Benjamin, a Hebrew born of Hebrews; as to the law, a Pharisee; as to zeal, a persecutor of the church; as to righteousness under the law, blameless" (see also Rom 11:1; Gal 1:13–14 also implicitly reveals his Pharisaic background). While Paul proudly announces this prominent Jewish background, he notes it only for the sake of contrast with what he has gained in Jesus Christ, as the next verse in Philippians indicates (3:7). We can conclude that Paul probably received a rather traditional Jewish upbringing in an urban environment within the context of a multicultural and multilingual society.

5. What kind of education did Paul receive?

Your question touches upon an area that has elicited considerable scholarly controversy. The Philippians passage I referred to in the previous question indicates that Paul had some sort of training in Jewish law from the perspective of the Pharisees. Paul clearly had some education. As a Jew he must have been familiar with Hebrew and Aramaic. As a citizen of a Greco-Roman city he also was familiar with Koinē (common) Greek, in which he wrote his letters. The real controversy has to do with how much and what kind of education Paul might have had.

Paul's own letters make no reference to any formal education. Apparently he could read and write (letters were normally dictated in Paul's day), but one can question his exact abilities. When concluding the Letter to the Galatians, for instance, Paul writes, "See what large letters I make when I am writing in my own hand!" (Gal 6:11). Does this mean that he could not write elegant script? Does it indicate that he had a limited formal education? All one can say is that Paul sometimes concluded his letters with personal writing (1 Cor 16:21).

Acts paints a different picture of Paul's education. In Acts Paul asserts that he was instructed "at the feet of Gamaliel" (22:3), presumably the famous Jewish rabbi, Gamaliel the Elder (a.k.a. Gamaliel I), who was a Pharisaic member of the Sanhedrin in Jerusalem in the middle of the first century A.D. (Acts 5:34). If this information is accurate, then Paul certainly had a formal education in a rabbinical setting. Curiously, although he emphasizes his own Pharisaic approach to the law, Paul nowhere mentions a formal education, let alone under the tutelage of a famous rabbi like Gamaliel. Paul's letters show evidence of his ability to think and to interpret scripture in a rabbinic fashion, but this alone does not confirm Paul's formal education. I think it best to conclude that while there is no need to doubt Acts' assertion of education under Gamaliel, there is also no proof of this.

More important is the evidence from Paul's letters. They show a real knowledge of Greco-Roman rhetorical style, especially in the use of a literary device, called the "diatribe." A diatribe is a rhetorical device, found in several different formats, in which questions are put forth (sometimes from an imaginary dialogue partner) that can then be refuted (see question 53). It was common to Cynic and Stoic philosophers in Paul's day. Good examples are found in Romans (e.g., Rom 2:1–6; 10:6–8). Further rhetorical evidence is found in the structure of some of the letters. Although scholars sometimes exaggerate that every letter of Paul can be structured according to Greek categories, there is sufficient evidence of some influences, especially in a letter like Galatians (see Hans Dieter Betz, *Galatians* [Hermeneia; Philadelphia: Fortress, 1979]) .

Paul's letters also reveal his knowledge of Jewish rabbinic interpretive practices. The rabbis had imaginative ways of applying their scriptures to new situations, and Paul demonstrates that he handles such interpretive moves with ease (see question 51).

To conclude, although our available evidence about Paul's formal education is somewhat limited, there can be no question that he was well educated and literate.

6. What really happened at Paul's conversion on the road to Damascus?

Paul himself left no written record that describes in detail what happened at his conversion. This may seem surprising, since Christians have traditionally viewed Paul's conversion as one of the archetypical conversions of the world. Artists throughout history have painted marvelous scenes of Paul falling from his horse and being blinded by a bright light. Influential as such images have been, Paul himself does not provide this kind of information. To get at your question we need to look at the difference between what Paul says and what the Acts of the Apostles indicates happened on the road to Damascus. The only two passages where Paul refers to Damascus do not relate to his conversion experience. He speaks of returning to Damascus after having spent time in Arabia (Gal 1:17). Elsewhere Paul recounts the story of his escape from the clutches of his opponents by being let down in a basket from a window in the wall (2 Cor 11:32–33; cf. Acts 9:23–25). Both of these passages concern his life after his conversion and do not give us further information.

Paul terms his own experience of conversion a "revelation" (Gal 2:2) or an "appearance" of the risen Lord (1 Cor 9:1; 15:8). These two expressions are as explicit as Paul comes to describing what he experienced. Note that he does not refer to Damascus in describing the event (though it is mentioned in Gal 1:17) nor does he give details that would pinpoint the circumstances and timing of it. The Greek words for revelation (*apokalypsis* = unveiling) and appearance (*ōphthē* = to be seen, to appear) do not give us the kind of historical data that your question seeks. Both convey a sense of the risen Lord making personal contact with Paul in a manner beyond human perception. In First Corinthians Paul insists that he is no less a recipient of a call from the risen Lord than other followers, some of whom also received post-resurrectional appearances (see 1 Cor 15:3–11). In other words, Paul's own account does not yield much specific historical information on his conversion, but it does assert that God revealed his Son to him, and this is what is important for Paul.

Acts presents a different picture. Everyone is familiar with the story in Acts 9:1–19 that recounts what happened to Paul on the road to Damascus. Although the story is told three times in

Acts (also in 22:6–16; 26:12–18) with slightly different details and emphases, the basic outline of the story is clear. Paul was underway to Damascus with permission from Jewish authorities in Jerusalem to arrest some followers of Jesus. He was blinded by a bright light, fell to the ground, and heard a voice that said, "Saul, Saul, why do you persecute me?" (9:4; 22:7; 26:14; the exact same Greek words in each case). The voice identifies itself with the words, "I am Jesus, whom you are persecuting." Then Paul is instructed to go to a believer named Ananias in order to be healed of his blindness and to be baptized.

There are significant symbolic elements in this story as recounted in Acts. Blindness and sight, darkness and light, and the meaning of the different sets of instruction given to Paul that he is to minister to the Gentiles all have symbolic value for the author of Acts. Even the threefold repetition of Paul's conversion indicates its importance in the overall plan of Acts. For these reasons, among others, some scholars rightly suggest that "call" or "commission" is a better label for Paul's experience than "conversion." They point to similarities with other prophetic call narratives whereby God calls a prophet to a specific mission (e.g., 1 Sam 3:10). Although I admit that it is awkward, I often use the double expression "conversion/call" to broaden the notion of Paul's dramatically transformed life.

In the end, we must admit that we do not know the actual historical details of Paul's conversion. Paul does not give us such details himself, and Acts may have its own theological concerns that overshadow the historical circumstances. Yet nothing inherently presented in the story of Acts contradicts what Paul says about his own conversion. It is most important to recognize that Paul's conversion/call was not a radical change in religions. Paul was born, lived, and died a Jew, albeit one who accepted Jesus as messiah. His so-called conversion was not a movement from Judaism to Christianity but a commissioning by the risen Lord Jesus, whom he accepted as messiah, to go preach to the Gentiles.

7. Why was Paul's name changed from Saul?

Your question expresses a common presumption that Paul's name was indeed changed. However, that may not be the case. In the OT we do find examples of name changes that signify an interior change of a person or a new stage in their lives. In Genesis, for example, God declares, "No longer shall your name be Abram, but your name shall be Abraham; for I have made you the ancestor of a multitude of nations" (Gen 17:5). This change in name not only signifies a special relationship with God but also makes a play on words as to the meaning of the new name (cf. also Sarai/Sarah [Gen 17:15] and Naomi/Mara [Ruth 1:20]). The name "Abraham" is said to mean "father of a multitude" for it evokes the Hebrew word for "many" (*rab*), recalling God's promise. Do we encounter a similar phenomenon in the case of Paul?

Note that in the letters of Paul the name "Saul" never occurs. Paul does not even use it in relation to his former life. He always refers to himself as "Paul." By the time Paul writes his letters, the only name he uses with his communities seems to be Paul. Most likely, this was his given name. Only in Acts do we encounter the dual names of Saul and Paul. Prior to the story of Paul's conversion in Acts 9, he is known simply as Saul (see Acts 7:58; 8:1–3; 9:1). Also note that after the conversion story, Acts still occasionally uses the name Saul (13:7,9), although most frequently the name Paul appears. More importantly, the only place in Acts where both names are used side by side is Acts 13:9, which simply says, "But Saul, also known as Paul…." This is the last time Acts uses the name "Saul"; thereafter, "Paul" alone is used, and Paul assumes a greater role in leadership of the missionary activity recounted in Acts. Yet it is remarkable that Acts attaches no special meaning to the designations but refers to them simply as dual names. Thus a more likely explanation for the two names Saul and Paul is not that a change occurred at or shortly after his conversion experience. Rather, Paul was a man who lived in two worlds. He came from Jewish parents who lived in the diaspora, that is, in the secular world outside of the Holy Land. His Jewish name, Saul, reflects this Jewish heritage. The name Paul, on the other hand, is the Greek equivalent that would have been used more commonly in the Greco-Roman society of Paul's day.

8. When, where, and how did Paul die?

You may remember that artists throughout history have often painted portraits of Paul leaning on or holding a sword, indicating the means of his death. Such artistic portrayal, however, does not necessarily convey accurate historical information. Neither Paul's letters nor Acts provide any specific account regarding the death of Paul. Acts narrates Paul's journey to Rome, as well as his captivity in Rome awaiting trial and judgment (Acts 27—28), but it does not recount Paul's death.

Ancient tradition indicates that Paul died a martyr's death by beheading in Rome in the early to mid-60s A.D. under the emperor Nero, around the same time that Peter was martyred. This tradition is based upon non-biblical sources, such as the First Letter of Clement (ca. A.D. 96)—the most important reference to the martyrdom of Paul—and the apocryphal Acts of Paul (ca. A.D. 185–95). However, there are clearly elements of religious exaggeration in the description of his death. There was a common tendency in early Christian writings to lace the description of martyrdoms with miraculous details that even early interpreters recognized as historically unreliable. Although there is no firm information about Paul's death, the ancient tradition of his beheading in Rome in the time of Nero (A.D. 62–64) fits well with the general outline of his life and ministry.

9. Why doesn't the Acts of the Apostles describe Paul's death?

Speculations about why an ancient biblical book does not mention a certain piece of information are fraught with dangers. One could say that Acts does not tell us of Paul's death because it was written before the actual event. This response is not applicable in this case because most scholars date Acts about two decades after Paul's death. Another reason could be that the author of Acts was simply unaware of Paul's death. This explanation, too, however, seems unlikely because Acts has such an intense interest in Paul that it would be difficult to imagine that the author would not have followed the story to its conclusion. Of course, it is also possible to speculate that Paul was never martyred, but as I indicated in the previous question, there is little reason to doubt the ancient tradition of his martyrdom. A more likely explanation for the absence is that the author has some theological purpose in mind. What might that be?

Let's take a moment to examine the conclusion of Acts. Acts 28:23–31 describes Paul in prison or more accurately under a kind of house arrest. In the face of some acceptance and some rejection of his preaching, Paul finally quotes to his Jewish audience the stern passage from Isaiah that sadly indicates that the chosen people refuse to see the truth or to hear it proclaimed to them (Isa 6:9–10). Paul concludes, "Let it be known to you then that this salvation of God has been sent to the Gentiles; they will listen" (Acts 28:28). Paul's last words confirm his initial call. The risen Lord had indicated that he was to be "an instrument whom I have chosen to bring my name before Gentiles and kings and before the people of Israel; I myself will show him how much he must suffer for the sake of my name" (Acts 9:15–16). The final verses of Acts conclude by summarizing Paul's ministry of proclaiming the Word of God "with all boldness and without hindrance" (Acts 28:31). I am suggesting that this type of conclusion to Acts may well serve a more hopeful purpose to Christian readers. It calls attention not to the act of martyrdom itself (that Luke's audience presumably knew) but to the necessity of boldly preaching God's Word in the face of any difficulties. It also summarizes how the Gentiles became the hearers of the Word and ultimately fashioned a new faith community.

10. But I thought that Luke wrote Acts. Wasn't he a companion of Paul, the beloved physician, who accompanied him on his journeys? Wouldn't he know all about Paul?

That has been the traditional explanation of why parts of Acts are written in the first-person plural, the "we-passages" (16:10–17; 20:5–15; 21:8–18; 27:1–28:16). It is possible that the author of Acts had some direct information from Paul or his companions. Luke or the author of Acts may have been a "sometime" companion of Paul. There are many details of Paul's story that can be verified by Paul's letters and by a knowledge of ancient geography. Some scholars have suggested that these passages constitute an eyewitness account to Paul's ministry because they were written by Luke, the beloved physician. Others, however, have raised serious questions about this theory. Note that these passages only encompass the latter part of the Book of Acts. Why are earlier sections on Paul's ministry not written in this fashion?

If the author of Luke-Acts was not, in fact, a companion of Paul, a possible explanation is that the we-passages are really a literary device used in ancient storytelling to enliven the narrative and to make it more realistic. The name Luke never occurs in the Acts of the Apostles, neither in the title nor in the body of the text. Within the letters of Paul the name Luke is found in Philemon 24 in a list of Paul's coworkers, and in two other letters whose Pauline authorship is uncertain. Second Timothy records Paul saying that "Only Luke is with me" (2 Tim 4:11). Only in Colossians do we find the expression "Luke the beloved physician," in a greeting that gives no further information as to his identity (Col 4:14). This passage does not say clearly who this Luke is. It never explicitly identifies him as a companion of Paul let alone say that this was the Luke who authored Acts. Luke was a common name at the time, and there is nothing specific to identify the beloved physician with the author of the only two-volume work in the NT. Some older theories used to detail specific medical vocabulary in Luke-Acts to verify that the author was indeed a physician. Newer studies have shown that such vocabulary is an illusion; Luke-Acts is no more specifically medical than any other NT writing.

Another difficulty with identifying the author of Acts with Luke the beloved physician is the viewpoint of Acts when compared with Paul's own letters. There are some tensions—perhaps due to perspective—when one compares the two. Some examples will illustrate. Acts portrays Paul as residing in Jerusalem and journeying to Damascus only to fulfill his duties prior to his conversion (Acts 8:1–3); Galatians, however, indicates that Paul resided in Damascus (Gal 1:17–18). Acts speaks of Paul and Barnabas assisting with famine relief with the church in Jerusalem (Acts 11:29–30); Galatians gives a different version of the sequence and rationale for Paul's journeys (Gal 1:17–2:1). A third example is the differing version of events at the Council of Jerusalem (Acts 15; Gal 2) that will be discussed in the next question. Acts shows Paul receiving the endorsement of Peter and James for his Gentile mission, while Galatians speaks of the need for Paul to stand up to these main leaders in the believing community. Finally, it is curious that Acts never mentions Paul writing letters, since that is the primary way in which he kept in touch with the communities he evangelized and the main way through which we have come to know Paul.

We could find other examples of disagreements between the two sources. For the most part the disagreements cannot be harmonized into one synthetic picture of what really happened. That is why questions can be raised about whether Acts is always accurate in its portrayal of Paul's life and ministry. If Luke was an eyewitness to the events narrated, then why is his perspective so different? The author of Acts, of course, has his own theological interests for telling Paul's story in his own way, but this does not totally resolve these tensions.

Most problematic for trying to defend the idea that Acts gives the testimony of an eyewitness account to the ministry of Paul are two other observations. Paul's speeches recorded in Acts closely resemble other speeches, such as those of Peter, Stephen,

and James in the same book. Scholars have shown the speeches of
Acts to be a collection of Lukan themes that recur over and over
again. One also should not miss that the author of Luke-Acts dis-
tances himself from an eyewitness account by admitting that he
relies on such firsthand accounts in order to restructure and retell
the story of Jesus and the early church (Luke 1:2; Acts 1:1).

In short, Paul had at least one companion named Luke who
was known to some of Paul's churches. He may or may not have
been, however, the author of Acts.

11. What was the Council of Jerusalem and what does it have to do with Paul?

The Council of Jerusalem designates a meeting of certain
leading followers of Jesus that is described in Acts 15:1–21. Acts
indicates that Paul was involved in this meeting because the primary issue was the mission to the Gentiles. Paul writes in Galatians 2:1–10 about such a meeting that appears to be the same
meeting Acts describes. The problem is that the two accounts
diverge in significant details.

Two issues appear in the story in Acts: circumcision and
dietary laws relating to meat deemed unclean because it is used in
pagan worship. The issue of circumcision clearly was a sensitive
issue among the early disciples of Jesus. For the Jews it was an
identity issue, for the Gentiles it was a barbaric practice. Once
Gentiles started to accept the gospel message and enter the community of disciples, the smoldering issue burst into a full-fledged
fire. According to Acts, after the testimony of Paul and Barnabas
at a public gathering of Christian leaders, two major figures in the
Jerusalem community, Simon Peter and James, testified. Both
voiced an opinion. They spoke in favor of relaxing some of the
restraints that others were trying to place upon the Gentile converts. Circumcision would not be required. They would be asked
simply to refrain from fornication and meat previously sacrificed
to idols.

Paul tells a different story. In his view, he went to Jerusalem to seek out a private meeting with certain key apostolic leaders, namely, Peter, James, and John. His Greek companion Titus was not compelled to be circumcised, but some dissenters stirred up a controversy to retain the practice of circumcision. Paul says that the three "acknowledged pillars" of the church gave him their blessing to proceed with his mission to the Gentiles just as they would continue working with the circumcised. A little later, though, Paul indicates that Peter reneged on the deal at Antioch (Gal 2:11–14). He acquiesced to pressure from those favoring circumcision and withdrew from table fellowship with the Gentiles.

Who has the more accurate view of what happened at this "council"? Was it public or private? Was it really about circumcision or about dietary regulations, or both? Did Peter and James fully approve the Gentile mission or only in a limited fashion? We cannot resolve such historical questions with ease. What we can say is that the Council of Jerusalem is an example of the early believing community trying to resolve a crisis by some sort of consultation. Even a late-comer like Paul could involve himself in such decisions.

12. If Paul was Jewish, how did he become a Roman citizen?

Most subjects of the Roman Empire remained citizens of their own countries or cities (cf. Acts 19:35), but it was not that unusual to be both Jewish and a Roman citizen in Paul's day. The Jews in the first century had gotten so used to being ruled by various foreign powers ever since the time of the Babylonian exile (6th century B.C.) that many had accommodated themselves to foreign rule, including citizenship. Roman citizenship, however, was not given automatically.

Paul nowhere indicates that he was a Roman citizen. Acts is again the source of this information. The first mention of this issue appears in Acts 16:37–38 when Paul is counted among a number of others as Roman citizens who have inappropriately been beaten and jailed. Paul explicitly admits to being a Roman citizen in Acts 22:27 (cf. 23:27). This status allows him to be treated with greater sensitivity and ultimately to appeal to Rome for a decision in his case. People could obtain Roman citizenship by means other than birth, such as being adopted into a prominent citizen's household or being freed as a slave. Scholars remain divided on the question. Although it is not historically implausible, we cannot be sure. If the tradition of Paul being beheaded is true (see question 8), it could be another indicator of Paul's Roman citizenship, as capital punishment for citizens included beheading but not torture or other cruel means (e.g., crucifixion) reserved for noncitizens.

13. Did Paul ever actually meet Jesus?

I would like to carefully rephrase your question. I presume that you mean, "Did Paul ever physically encounter Jesus of Nazareth?" You may be aware of the distinction that scholars often make between the "historical Jesus," "the real Jesus," and the "risen Christ" (see John. P. Meier, *A Marginal Jew: Rethinking the Historical Jesus,* Vol. I [New York: Doubleday, 1991], pp. 21–40). Without getting sidetracked into the details of the search for the "historical Jesus," I should indicate why the distinction is important for understanding Paul. Paul apparently did not meet Jesus of Nazareth in person. But Paul would insist that he had encountered Jesus of Nazareth (the expression "of Nazareth" does not appear in Paul's letters) as the risen Christ. Paul especially insists on this point in First Corinthians. He asks forcefully, "Have I not seen Jesus our Lord?" (1 Cor 9:1). In his famous passage on the resurrection he testifies that he, no less than the other apostles, has been privileged to "see" the risen Lord whose call authenticates his position as an apostle (1 Cor 15:8–10). He also asserts that he received his commission by "revelation" from the risen Jesus himself (Gal 1:12). For Paul, one does not need to have known Jesus of Nazareth in person during his earthly ministry to have a valid encounter with him.

Another facet of your question is to examine carefully the language Paul uses about Jesus. Notice, for instance, that his favorite expression is "Christ Jesus" (Rom 3:24; 1 Cor 1:1; 4:15; Gal 2:4; 3:26,28; etc.), rather than our customary "Jesus Christ" that literally means Jesus Messiah. The notion of messiah (Hebrew *mašiah* = "anointed one"), of course, derives from a Jewish background. In the OT it designates kings and prophets who were anointed by God to serve the people (Pss 2:2; 89:21). Later it figured in Christian thought as it was applied, through a complex history that we cannot explain here, to Jesus as messiah or "the Christ." With the exception of a few scattered references in the NT, Paul is the only one to use the expression "Christ Jesus" dozens of times. Paul never uses the term "Christ" with the definite article (i.e., "the messiah") except in Romans 9:5, where the term is more generic in the context of a list of God's gifts to the Israelites. Perhaps by Paul's time, the word "Christ" (from Greek, *christos* = messiah, anointed one) had already begun to take on the characteristics of a name rather than a title. Paul gives this new impetus by transposing the words and placing "messiah" before Jesus' proper name so that, in effect, Christ functions more as a name than a title (cf. Matt 16:16; Mark 8:29; 1 John 2:22; 5:1). For Paul, Jesus is Christ by virtue of his death and resurrection (1 Cor 15:3–4). That is why Paul can claim to be no less an apostle than others who were called by Jesus during his earthly ministry.

This response essentially assures us that all succeeding generations of Jesus' disciples, including ourselves, can be called by Christ Jesus. We, no less than our predecessors, have the opportunity to encounter the risen Lord just as Paul did.

14. Why did Paul persecute Christians?

Your question has a delicate side that I would like to respect; namely, sensitivity between Jews and Christians in our own day.

We should not interject our modern sensitivities into the ancient biblical texts. Paul's involvement in the persecution of followers of Jesus should not be seen in an isolated fashion. After the death and resurrection of Jesus, most who believed Jesus to be the Jewish messiah remained faithful to their Jewish roots. There was no firm distinction between Judaism and Christianity until it developed later. Believers continued to attend synagogues and practice their faith. As was the case with Paul, they remained Jewish. In time, however, differences between Jews who accepted Jesus as the messiah and those who did not became intolerable. Inevitable tensions arose that led to acts of intolerance and even persecutions. Eventually, these believers in Jesus left the synagogue and became known as Christians (cf. Acts 11:26). (For the sake of convention, I use the term even of believers in Paul's day.)

Already in Paul's day such tensions appeared. His letters clearly admit to involvement in persecutions, but without describing what that entailed. Paul admits, "You have heard, no doubt, of my earlier life in Judaism. I was violently persecuting the church of God and was trying to destroy it. I advanced in Judaism beyond many among my people of the same age, for I was far more zealous for the traditions of my ancestors" (Gal 1:13–14; see also 1 Cor 15:9). This attitude would be consistent with that of other Pharisees who sought to retain the purity of Judaism. Note that a similar connection between Paul's zeal for his former faith and his involvement in anti-Christian persecution appears also in Philippians 3:6. In my opinion, this zeal is most likely the reason for Paul's participation in such persecutions. He was very zealous and perceived the Christian movement as a threat to Judaism as he understood it at that time. From this vantage point some scholars rightly point to Paul's continuity with other great figures in Israel's history who tried zealously to protect Judaism from being corrupted by Gentile impurity and pagan practices (e.g., Phinehas, Num 25:6–13; and Mattathias, 1 Macc 1:27; 2:50).

Acts also indicates that Paul was zealous in his former life. Acts even places Paul at the death of the first martyr, Stephen, the day "a severe persecution began against the church in Jerusalem" (Acts 8:1; cf. 9:1–2). But note that Acts places the persecutions in the larger context that Israel had frequently persecuted prophets whom God had sent (Acts 7:52).

15. Why was Paul so readily accepted into the Christian community when it was common knowledge that he had once persecuted them?

In fact, Paul may not have been so readily accepted into the Christian community as your question presumes. Acts indicates, for instance, that there was fear and anxiety on the part of some believers. Ananias, to whom Paul is sent after his conversion/call, protests the Lord's request to receive Paul with the words, "Lord, I have heard from many about this man, how much evil he has done to your saints in Jerusalem; and here he has authority from the chief priests to bind all who invoke your name" (9:13–14). When Paul arrives in Jerusalem, Acts also portrays a negative response: "…they were all afraid of him, for they did not believe that he was a disciple" (9:26). Paul himself admits to his reputation as a persecutor and that this was originally the only way some churches knew about him: "…and I was still unknown by sight to the churches of Judea that are in Christ; they only heard it said, 'The one who was formerly persecuting us is now proclaiming the faith he once tried to destroy'" (Gal 1:22–23).

Reading carefully between the lines one gets a sense in Paul's own letters that the situation was not entirely hospitable toward him. Many passages intimate a defensive tone that indicates that he had to fight hard to be accepted. This phenomenon is technically called apologetic. One such apologetic passage shows Paul pleading with the church at Corinth that he founded: "Am I not free? Am I not an apostle? Have I not seen Jesus our Lord? Are you not my work in the Lord? If I am not an apostle to others, at least I am to you; for you are the seal of my apostleship in the Lord. This is my defense to those who would examine me"

(1 Cor 9:1–3). Elsewhere Paul also strongly affirms his role in the church by reminding his readers that his mission is not his own or derivative of others but commissioned directly by God (Gal 1:1, 12). Paul can admit his unworthiness in this task, as in 1 Corinthians 15:9; he acknowledges, "For I am the least of the apostles, unfit to be called an apostle, because I persecuted the church of God." These apologetic motifs hint that Paul did not find it easy to integrate into the Christian community. Although many other factors influenced this predicament, his past history was likely one of them.

16. Why is Paul called an apostle when he wasn't one of the twelve apostles?

You have obviously noticed that Paul calls himself an apostle, yet as I pointed out in a prior question, he did not have personal contact with Jesus of Nazareth in Jesus' lifetime, nor was he a member of Jesus' inner circle of apostles. The short response to your question is that the risen Jesus appeared to Paul and called him to be an apostle (1 Cor 1:1; Gal 1:1). To respond to your question in more detail, let's review some basic NT vocabulary.

In the NT the word "apostle" (Greek *apostolos* = sent one) and the word "disciple" (Greek *mathētēs* = learner, student) can be used interchangeably at times. Matthew formally designates the twelve closest followers of Jesus "apostles" (Matt 10:2) when he lists them, yet throughout the rest of the Gospel they are called "the disciples." In Luke-Acts, however, a distinction exists between the labels "apostle" and "disciple." For Luke the word "apostle" belongs almost exclusively to the Twelve. So important is the symbolic presentation of the twelve apostles that Acts describes the choice of another to take the place of Judas the betrayer (Acts 1:21–26). The one exception is Acts 14:14 where Paul is also designated an apostle along with Barnabas. Otherwise Luke restricts the word to the Twelve. (Note that Luke-Acts never employs the singular form of the word. Is this because he always views the Twelve as an unbroken group symbolically representing Jesus' reconstitution of the twelve tribes of Israel?) It is interesting to note that Paul never uses the term "disciple" in his letters. He only uses the term "apostle." He applies it to himself as well as to other key figures among the early followers of Jesus. He uses the word "apostle" many times, but only once does he mention the "twelve" as a group (1 Cor 15:5). Instead Paul uses the term to describe anyone whom Jesus Christ has both called and sent on a mission to evangelize the world. Paul obviously sees apostles in a prominent place in the Christian community. He places apostles first in the list of ministries (1 Cor 12:28). He recognizes and honors the roles of prominent apostles who have preceded him. He frequently refers to himself as an apostle, especially in certain contexts that emphasize his authority (Rom 1:1; 2 Cor 1:1; Gal 1:1). Yet Paul also can use the term apologetically or sometimes with sarcasm. When he describes his first trip to Jerusalem to see Peter and James the brother of Lord, he indicates that he did not meet with any other apostle. He compares himself as apostle "to the Gentiles" with Peter who is "apostle to the circumcised" (Gal 2:8). When he apparently felt incensed at a derogatory comparison between himself and other apostles (most likely not the Twelve), he could cry out "I think that I am not in the least inferior to these super-apostles" (2 Cor 11:5; cf. 12:11).

In summary, Paul is proud to call himself an apostle because he feels strongly that Jesus Christ has designated him such no less than the original apostles. He, no less than they, has done wondrous deeds (2 Cor 12:12; cf. Acts 19:11–12). From a pastoral perspective, isn't this significant for our own situation centuries removed from the events in the life of Jesus? Paul's position regarding apostleship means that we, no less than the original apostles, can share in the apostolic mission of the Church.

17. Does modern archaeology tell us anything about Paul? What about the Dead Sea Scrolls? Do they help us understand Paul?

Modern archaeology does not so much tell us about Paul himself as about the world he and his congregations inhabited. Archaeologists have done extensive excavations in the Holy Land, at Ephesus in Turkey, at Corinth and Philippi in Greece, and many other places that have given us windows into the world of the first century. There is no substitute for visiting these sites, but pictures, slides, and videos help to envision the environment of Paul's world. One can see vividly the setting of the market-places (technically called *agora*) where daily life was lived. Ancient coins and inscriptions have been found that also flesh out aspects of daily existence in the first century. The foundations of ancient buildings such as synagogues and temples, or houses of the wealthy, and apartment dwellings of the working class, give some sense of perspective. Some of these have provided clues about the nature of "house churches" among the early followers of Jesus (see question 33). In Corinth one can see the foundations of the judgment seat (*bēma*) where the proconsul Gallio may well have interrogated Paul on the occasion of some Jewish opposition (Acts 18:12–17). Determining Gallio's term of office (ca. A.D. 50–51 or 51–52), in fact, has also helped to date the earliest letter of Paul (1 Thess).

One has to be cautious about making extravagant claims about the value of some of these sites. A tour guide in Philippi once explained to our tour group that a certain small room at an excavated site was surely the location of Paul's imprisonment in Philippi. Actually, there was no real evidence to verify this. It could just as easily have been a storage area. The point is that archaeology helps to recreate the ambience of Paul's world. It has not thus far given detailed information about Paul's personal life. Archaeology has essentially affirmed that his roots are firmly planted within Judaism under the influence of the Hellenistic-Roman world.

The Dead Sea Scrolls also play a role in helping to flesh out Paul's world. You will recall that a shepherd boy discovered them in 1947 while tending his flocks near the Dead Sea. They are sometimes called the Qumran scrolls, a reference to the site where they were found near the Wadi Qumran. Over the years, most of the scrolls have been published. Thousands of tiny fragments have been deciphered. These Jewish documents date some two centuries before Paul. They are not, however, totally irrelevant to Paul. Scholars do not propose any direct connection between Paul and the Qumran scrolls or the community that produced them. Yet several theological concepts prominent in Paul can be found in the scrolls as well (see Jerome Murphy-O'Connor and James H. Charlesworth, eds., *Paul and the Dead Sea Scrolls* [New York: Crossroad, 1990]). Examples include the following notions:

* human beings are sinful;
* only God can make people righteous; they cannot "earn" salvation;
* God has a divine plan of salvation for the world;
* God's plan predestines what will happen;
* the law (torah) is important but also has limitations.

Naturally, unlike the inhabitants of Qumran who expected a royal messiah and a priestly messiah, Paul acknowledged Jesus as the long-awaited messiah of Israel. What the similarities tell us is that Paul was very much at home in the Jewish thought world that shaped his era. This information has helped scholars to reevaluate the strong Jewish background of Paul's letters.

18. What is "apocalyptic" and how does it relate to Paul's letters?

The word "apocalyptic" (from Greek *apokalypsis* = unveiling, revelation) refers both to a type of literature found in the Bible and to a mindset or outlook that undergirds these writings. Examples of this kind of biblical literature include the Book of Daniel in the OT and the Book of Revelation in the NT. In addition, parts of other books of the Bible exhibit characteristics of apocalyptic, such as Zechariah 12–14, Ezekiel 38–39, and Mark 13. Apocalyptic literature arose in the late prophetic period of the OT. Typically, such literature arises in contexts of severe persecution or times when one's religion or very existence are under serious threat. Characteristics of such literature include the following:

- *dualism*—a belief that good and evil are caught in a desperate cosmic battle. This is often expressed in sharply contrasting imagery or symbolism, like light and darkness or utter damnation and salvation. While they necessarily overlap, there is also a contrast between the two "ages": the present age is passing away; there is a new age to come in which God's victory over evil will be finally secured. At times, the new age is preceded by an interim period in which the righteous will have to suffer before the final victory is accomplished.

- *determinism*—a belief that God is ultimately in charge of human history and has determined its final outcome. Included in such a notion can be the idea of predestination, the belief that God has preordained the outcome of history. In the apocalyptic view, appearances can be deceiving. Though the situation can seem dire and hopeless, adherents to an apocalyptic view believe that God will be victorious in the end.

- *eschatological judgment*—Closely tied to the previous concept is this idea that God will finally vindicate the righteous and condemn the unrighteous. At the end of time (*eschaton* = Greek "end time"; from which is derived the adjective "eschatological") God will sit in judgment over all humanity, and whoever was an enemy of God in life will get their comeuppance, while the faithful "elect" will be rewarded with everlasting life.

- *urgency*—coupled with the above notions, the idea that the world as we know it is quickly coming to an end and therefore there is an urgent need to pay attention to remaining faithful in the midst of trials and to adhere to what is right. Thus there is a strong exhortation to remain vigilant and resistant to backsliding.

- *stringent ethical teaching*—the belief that maintaining a faithful and righteous life, even in the midst of suffering or persecution, is required for those who want to be vindicated by God at the end of time.

Such a worldview is found in various elements of Judaism. The community at Qumran, for instance, exhibits features of an apocalyptic world view. So corrupt did they think the Judaism of their day was, and so contaminated by Gentile influences, that they fled to the Dead Sea to preserve an authentic Jewish faith. The NT also exhibits characteristics of apocalyptic. Indeed, most scholars believe that Jesus himself was influenced by apocalyptic thought. His teachings reflect such an outlook (e.g., Mark 13; Matt 24–25).

The apocalyptic connection to Paul is also important. Most scholars recognize that many of Paul's letters contain apocalyptic elements that help to explain the urgency and stringent character of his message (see J. Christiaan Beker, *Paul's Apocalyptic Gospel: The Coming Triumph of God* [Philadelphia: Fortress, 1982]). In particular, as we shall see below in Part Six, Paul's apocalyptic and eschatological outlook strongly influenced his ethical teachings. Paul clearly believes that the end times are near (1 Cor 7:31; Phil 4:5; 1 Thess 5:2, though he refuses to speculate as to the exact time line) and that there is an urgency to his message. He also believes that God is in charge of human history, has predestined its outcome (Rom 8:28–30), and will ultimately be victorious (Rom 8:18–25; 1 Cor 15:20–28). For him, there is a cosmic battle being waged between good and evil forces, and thus he calls his communities to live in light rather than darkness, to be children of day rather than night (Rom 13:12; 2 Cor 6:14; 1 Thess 5:5), and to remain faithful to the gospel he proclaimed. The present age that is under the power of evil forces is passing away and will be succeeded by a new age in which righteousness will reign (1 Cor 2:6–9;Gal 1:4; Rom 12:2). The letters that fall into the Pauline tradition likewise show considerable influence from apocalyptic thought (e.g., Eph 5:8–9). Paul also sometimes speaks of revelatory visions that are common to apocalyptic literature and that reveal God's will (e.g., 2 Cor 12:1–7), but he warns against getting too caught up in such speculative experiences.

In sum, Paul's apocalyptic worldview, consonant with his Jewish background, impacts on much of his thought, including his theology, his spirituality, and his ethics. As we read Paul's letters, it is wise to keep an eye out for such influences, for they can help place Paul's thought in its proper context.

Two

Paul the Person

19. Everyone knows that Paul was a tentmaker. What was that job like?

We learn about Paul being a tentmaker in Acts. He himself never mentions specifically his line of work. Acts reveals that Paul worked in tentmaking with Aquila and Priscilla, colleagues whom he encountered in Corinth.

> After this Paul left Athens and went to Corinth. There he found a Jew named Aquila, a native of Pontus, who had recently come from Italy with his wife Priscilla, because Claudius had ordered all Jews to leave Rome. Paul went to see them, and, because he was of the same trade, he stayed with them, and they worked together—by trade they were tentmakers. (Acts 18:1–3)

There is no reason to doubt the basic information from Acts that Paul was a tentmaker. His home province in Asia Minor, Cilicia, was famous for a cloth made from goat hair *(cilicium)* that was often used in the production of tents. Sailors and soldiers frequently needed such tents in their work. It is also possible that Paul worked in the production of leather tents. These were likewise used in the Hellenistic world. Paul's work at this trade in Corinth fits well with the context. Corinth was situated near the site of the Isthmian games that were held in years when the Olympics were not held. Many visitors would come to the isthmus near Corinth for these games. Tents were a requisite for the athletes as well as for the tourists.

Tentmaking was hard physical labor. What is remarkable about Paul is that he insisted on doing physical labor in the midst of his evangelizing ministry. He considers physical labor one of the aspects of apostolic ministry, even though one might grow weary of it (1 Cor 4:12). He strongly advises his communities

41

about the necessity of physical work (1 Thess 4:11; 2 Thess 3:10–12). He also indicates that he does so to make the gospel available free of charge to all who would receive it (1 Cor 9:18). He reminds the Thessalonians that he purposefully did physical labor so as not to be a burden to them.

> You remember our labor and toil, brothers and sisters; we worked night and day, so that we might not burden any of you while we proclaimed to you the gospel of God. (1 Thess 2:9)

At Corinth he also hints that he worked along with other apostles (1 Cor 9:6, 15–18). Only at Philippi does Paul indicate that, for a time, he may have changed his normal pattern of working for a living while proclaiming the gospel. There he says that the reason was an illness. One of the reasons for writing the Letter to the Philippians is to commend them for taking care of him during his recovery and for sending him money when he left Philippi and moved on to Thessalonica (Phil 4:14–18). Even then, one gets the impression that Paul was a little embarrassed to take their charity (Phil 4:10–13).

In short, Paul was quite satisfied with working for a living after his commission. It is not clear whether he started this profession as a venture in tandem with his ministry, as a consequence of his call, or whether he had always been allied to it. In any case, he insisted on working and on not taking advantage of his ministry. He did not want to subsist off others for the sake of the gospel, although he humbly accepted assistance when he needed it.

20. Was Paul ever married? Did he have children?

There is no solid evidence in the scriptures or outside of them that Paul was married. Therefore, he did not likely have any children. But your question raises a serious point regarding how Paul fit into his own culture. In Paul's day almost all Jewish males married. It would have been quite unusual, but not unprecedented, to remain unmarried. If Paul were married, it would be difficult to explain why his wife would never once be referred to either in the Acts of the Apostles or in his own letters. He frequently mentions women, so why not his own wife? Was he perhaps widowed? Given his desire to protect the bond of marriage it is unlikely that he abandoned his wife and family at the beginning of his ministry (1 Cor 7:12–24). I want to take a look at two key passages where Paul speaks of these matters.

The primary evidence that Paul himself was unmarried comes from 1 Corinthians 7:7–8: "I wish that all were as I myself am. But each has a particular gift from God, one having one kind and another a different kind. To the unmarried and the widows I say that it is well for them to *remain unmarried as I am*" (my emphasis). The context for the passage is important. In this section of First Corinthians Paul is addressing an issue of sexuality and marriage that the Corinthians themselves have brought to Paul (1 Cor 7:1). He wishes to limit cases of sexual immorality. In vv. 2—6 Paul responds that marriage involves both the "conjugal rights" of each party and, by mutual agreement for a time perhaps, sexual abstinence. Most important is that monogamy be safeguarded. He then labels his perspective a "concession" rather than a "command." I would also emphasize another aspect of Paul's position concerning marriage and celibacy in this section of First Corinthians (chap. 5—7): He conditions everything that he has to say about the matter with his apocalyptic view that "…the present form of this world is passing away" (7:31). Therefore, whatever state people are in, his advice is: Stay that way! Don't cause yourself more anxiety by trying to change from one state to another. Since he believed that the return of Jesus Christ in judgment was just around the corner (see 7:29), it was more important to live in the present while anticipating the transformation of God's kingdom that was to come. Within this context he views each of these ways of life as a gift *(charisma)* appropriate to each individual.

Some have suggested that 1 Corinthians 9:5 indicates that Paul was married. "Do we not have the right to be accompanied by a believing wife (Greek literally = 'a sister as a wife'), as do the other apostles and the brothers of the Lord and Cephas?" Most of the apostles apparently were married, and the Gospels speak of Peter's mother-in-law (Mark 1:30). But I do not think that this Corinthian passage implies that Paul himself was married. Rather, the passage is apologetic (note the word "defense" in 9:3), part of the defense of his apostleship. Note that he speaks in the plural "we," thus speaking for himself and Barnabas (9:6). What he is insisting on is not that he is married but that he and his colleagues retain the right to marriage, just as all the other apostles. To interpret it as an admission of marriage does not fit with his clear statement of celibacy in 1 Corinthians 7.

21. It sounds like he believed that celibacy was a better way of life. Is this true?

Your impression is a common one, but I think it is a little simplistic. On the one hand, Paul seems to place a higher value on celibacy as compared with marriage precisely in those passages we mentioned in the previous question (1 Cor 5—7). Several statements give this impression:

- 7:28: Married people will experience "distress in this life."
- 7:32–34: Married people will have "divided interests" with regard to their families and the Lord.
- 7:38: One who marries does "well" but one who refrains from marriage does "better."
- 7:39–40: Widows are better off remaining single.

But other passages give a different impression, one that honors marriage:

- 7:3: Sex within marriage is a right and privilege for both parties.
- 7:11–15: Marriage should remain indissoluble except under special circumstances.
- 7:16: Spouses might assist the salvation of their unbelieving partners.
- 7:28, 36: Marriage is not sinful.

We cannot resolve the issue by placing the statements on some sort of interpretational scale to see which side tips the balance. We can, however, place them in the wider context of Paul's plea that "...each of you lead the life that the Lord has assigned, to which God called you. This is my rule in all the churches....In whatever condition you were called, brothers and sisters, there remain with God" (1 Cor 7:17, 24). Paul does not limit this rule to the status of being married or single. He applies it broadly to whether one is circumcised or uncircumcised, a slave or a free person. Regardless of your position in life, Paul calls for the status quo because this life will soon be transformed by the coming of God's kingdom.

This broader context is important so that we do not misconstrue what Paul is saying in our own day. The church teaches that *all* are called to holiness. Being celibate does not necessarily mean one is holier than noncelibates. This position fits with Paul's understanding that all are called to "unhindered devotion to the Lord" (1 Cor 7:35). But Paul is also a realist. If people have difficulty holding their sexual desires in check, then he encourages them to marry, "For it is better to marry than to be aflame with passion" (1 Cor 7:9). Yet he knows that marriage can provide distractions and produce anxieties that can conflict with proper devotion to God. He conceives of the celibate life as less distracted even if he acknowledges that celibates, too, can be anxious. In my judgment, then, it is too simplistic to say that Paul thought celibacy was better than marriage.

22. What was Paul's "thorn in the flesh"?

The passage you are referring to is found in Second Corinthians where Paul writes:

> Therefore, to keep me from being too elated, a thorn was given me in the flesh, a messenger of Satan to torment me, to keep me from being too elated. Three times I appealed to the Lord about this, that it would leave me, but he said to me, "My grace is sufficient for you, for power is made perfect in weakness." So, I will boast all the more gladly of my weaknesses, so that the power of Christ may dwell in me. (2 Cor 12:7–9)

Theories abound concerning the exact meaning of the expression, "a thorn was given me in the flesh." First, I would emphasize that the context of the passage reveals Paul describing in some detail his personal experience of visions and revelations. Such experiences could lead to personal boasting, but Paul says that the Lord kept him humble by means of this "messenger of Satan," that is, the thorn. Clearly it represents something negative. Was it something physical? Scholars have long speculated that Paul was afflicted with some physical ailment. Specific possibilities include recurrent malaria, epilepsy, a speech impediment, a limp, or the results of beatings that he received at various times in the service of the gospel. Others suggest the problem was a mental or a spiritual struggle, such as severe depression, doubts about his faith or his mission to the Gentiles, sufferings in general, the constant badgering of his enemies, or a specific opponent.

Of all the suggestions, the notion of a speech defect or a defective ability in rhetorical skill is most intriguing. In the same letter Paul speaks of being ridiculed for his physical presence and for his speaking ability: "For they say, 'His letters are weighty and strong, but his bodily presence is weak, and his speech contemptible'" (2 Cor 10:10). I have often wondered what Paul's speaking abilities may have been like. Maybe he wasn't that effective a preacher. (See the humorous story of Eutychus in Acts 20:9–12.)

Frankly the exact meaning is unknown. The word "flesh" does not necessarily imply a physical ailment. It could be a Hebraic way of speaking of his total person. If Paul does not tell his readers explicitly what he means, he nonetheless indicates its importance. God is the one in charge of life. Paul's weakness makes him all the more aware of his utter dependence upon God. Despite his personal sufferings, God's grace is sufficient for him to be effective in his ministry. He is not worried. Whatever afflictions he has, his strength comes from God alone rather than his own abilities.

23. Why does Paul seem so proud of his sufferings as a Christian?

Your question touches upon an important area of Paul's theology as much as it involves the personality of Paul. I would caution about the use of the word "proud." We should not think that Paul is puffed up with self-importance because of his sufferings. It is true that he sometimes goes on at length about everything he has endured in the performance of his mission. In each one of his letters he mentions sufferings in one aspect or another, sometimes with extensive catalogues of specific sufferings he has undergone. A good example is found in Second Corinthians when he compares himself to some of the other apostles:

> Are they ministers of Christ? I am talking like a madman—I am a better one: with far greater labors, far more imprisonments, with countless floggings, and often near death. Five times I have received from the Jews the forty lashes minus one. Three times I was beaten with rods. Once I received a stoning. Three times I was shipwrecked; for a night and a day I was adrift at sea; on frequent journeys, in danger from rivers, danger from bandits, danger from my own people, danger from Gentiles, danger in the city, danger in the wilderness, danger at sea, danger from false brothers and

sisters; in toil and hardship, through many a sleepless night,
hungry and thirsty, often without food, cold and naked. And,
besides other things, I am under daily pressure because of
my anxiety for all the churches. (2 Cor 11:23–28; see also 1
Cor 4:11–13; 2 Cor 12:10)

This "hardship list" can sound arrogant in our ears. That is not
what Paul means by it. He believes that being called as an apostle
of Jesus Christ will necessarily entail some sort of suffering. Just
as Jesus suffered in the course of his ministry, so will his disciples
suffer in the course of theirs (cf. Matt 10:24–25). Paul views such
abuse as an apostolic "red badge of courage," a sign that one has
made sacrifices in order to remain faithful to the calling of a true
apostle. He sometimes uses extremely strong language when
describing these sufferings. Disciples, he says, "…become like
the rubbish of the world, the dregs of all things, to this very day"
(1 Cor 4:13), and they are "treated as imposters" (2 Cor 6:8).
They frequently undergo beatings and imprisonments, hatred, and
rejection. This is the price one pays to follow Jesus. He firmly
believes that undergoing such experiences helps to conform our
lives to Christ while also building up the church (Phil 3:10; 2
Cor 1:6; 4:10).

I emphasize that Paul does not go overboard in suggesting
that Christians should seek out physical hardships. This perspective occasionally dominated a later understanding of martyrdom.
Paul emphasizes that if suffering comes our way because of our
commitment to Jesus Christ, it is not only natural but will also
strengthen our faith.

A related aspect is Paul's use of the verb "boast" and its
cognates. Paul frequently speaks of boasting, sometimes in relation to suffering. "[W]e also boast in our sufferings, knowing
that suffering produces endurance, and endurance produces
character, and character produces hope…" (Rom 5:3–4). Paul is
not speaking of boasting in the sense of inflating or broadcast-
ing one's own achievements. He often condemns such selfish
boasting as inappropriate (1 Cor 5:6; cf. 13:4). The boasting of

which he speaks is "boasting in the Lord" (1 Cor 1:31; 15:31; 2 Cor 10:17), that is, what God has done through the ministry of Paul and the work of his communities. He considers boasting of one's weaknesses and sufferings to be the only proper boasting of a believer (2 Cor 12:5, 9; Gal 6:14). The only other boasting he permits himself to do is in relation to the success of his communities in their tireless faith. He occasionally boasts of their achievements to bolster their sense of worth and to serve as an encouragement to others (2 Cor 7:4; 9:3; Phil 4:15–16). That is why boasting in this sense can lead to hope in the Christian community.

24. Why does Paul tell his readers to "imitate" him? Isn't that a bit arrogant?

Paul frequently speaks of imitation in his letters, but I would not categorize it as arrogance. For one thing, Paul uses a broader notion of imitation than the mere copying of his own actions. In First Thessalonians Paul commends the community because "you became imitators of *us and of the Lord*" (1 Thess 1:6; my emphasis). The plural includes his companions, Silvanus and Timothy (1 Thess 1:1), who accompanied him on many of his journeys and who were two of Paul's trusted coworkers. He also challenges others to imitate the example of other communities ("the churches of God in Christ Jesus that are in Judea," 1 Thess 2:14) in the way that they have received the gospel message. Of course, Paul also refers to the imitation of himself with regard to the Christian way of life (1 Cor 4:16; 11:1; Phil 3:17). Note that Paul places the imitation of himself in line with his imitation of the Lord Jesus (Phil 3:17). He insists that he has tried to imitate Jesus by his willingness to suffer for the sake of the faith and by keeping focused on the primary goal of Christian living; namely, the attainment of the kingdom of heaven. Paul's notion of imitation is indeed a type of modeling. Human beings need to have models set before them to emulate. True imitation is one of the greatest compliments that can be paid to someone. Paul does not believe he can provide a model on his own (Phil 3:13) but that God has facilitated his ability to model righteous behavior to his communities. He sees this idea of imitation as a type of parental guidance just as parents (hopefully) provide good modeling to their children (see 1 Cor 4:14–17).

Is this an arrogant kind of model? I don't think so. Instead, Paul tries to draw attention to the way in which Christians learn proper attitudes of faith and correct moral behavior. Imitation must go beyond simply "do as I say." It must reflect the ability to "do as I do." Paul believes he has correctly modeled both the attitudes and behavior that embody the proper life of a disciple.

25. How did Paul relate to the other apostles?

As I have already pointed out, Paul had some difficulty being accepted by the other apostles. He also felt that it was necessary to defend his right to be an apostle. In First Corinthians Paul mentions various sets of apostles in the list of people to whom the risen Lord appeared. One should take notice of the order of the appearances (1 Cor 15:5–8):

- first to Cephas
- the Twelve
- five hundred brothers and sisters at one time
- James
- all the apostles
- last of all to me, least of the apostles

Paul affirms that he encountered two people who appear in this list, Cephas (the Greek version of Simon Peter's Aramaic name, *Kēphas* [= rock]) and James, the brother of the Lord. After his conversion/call Paul went to Jerusalem and met with Cephas for two weeks (Gal 1:18), but he says he did not meet with any other apostle other than James the brother of the Lord (Gal 1:19). He also met with another apostle, John, who is mentioned in Gal 2:9 as one of the pillars of the church. He participated in the decision to allow Paul to carry on a mission to the Gentiles. It may seem curious to us that little historical information is known about the apostles. Simon Peter was certainly prominent in the early church, and James the brother of the Lord was known as the head of the Jerusalem church. Paul indicates that some colleagues or followers of James were the ones who, in Antioch, caused Peter to back off from the agreement to eat with the Gentiles (Gal 2:12). Paul had contempt for this action as hypocrisy. He also associates James with the "circumcision party," probably referring to those who wanted to retain the requirement of circumcision for Gentile converts.

In the list of the aforementioned resurrection appearances, there are some curiosities. For instance, are the Twelve a separate group from the "all the apostles"? Are the five hundred all considered apostles or do they fit into a different category? Note that Paul comes last and is contrasted with Cephas who comes first. Paul boldly says that he opposed Peter to his face over the hypocritical actions in Antioch (Gal 2:14). Paul was not unwilling to challenge a major apostolic figure, the one whom the Gospels portray as the chief spokesman for the twelve apostles. It is evident, then, that Paul had some tense relations with some of the major apostolic leaders in the early church. Even Acts hints that Paul had some difficulties relating to the apostolic leadership, but Acts also paints a rosier picture of how the church smoothed out such difficulties. Contrary to Paul's own letters, Peter and James come across as having encouraged the move toward the Gentiles (Acts 11:4–18; 15:6–21). Given the tendency of Acts to gloss over some aspects of disunity in the early church, I think Paul had some serious difficulties relating to the other apostles. He had to fight hard for the recognition that he felt was rightfully his by virtue of his divine call to minister to the Gentiles. I imagine, however, that he respected them for their position provided they did not oppose his gospel message.

26. Can you say more about the relationship between Peter and Paul? Peter was very important in the early church, yet sometimes Paul seems to have been more powerful. How could that be?

Peter obviously held a prominent place in several communities of the early church (cf. Matt 16:17–19; Mark 3:16; Acts 2:14–36), and the NT in general testifies to Peter's prominence. Peter's role was one of authority, promoting unity and speaking for the apostles. Paul respects that position and calls attention to it. However, it would be a mistake to think that Peter functioned as a universal leader in the early church in the way, for instance, Catholics now view the Petrine ministry of the pope, which evolved into its distinctive contemporary shape over time. Remember that Paul founded most of the believing communities to which he wrote letters. He had a special devotion to them as they did to him. His own role in their midst was an authoritative one. In this regard Peter would not have functioned as authoritatively in those communities as Paul himself did. On the other hand, Paul understands Peter's privileged position within Christian history. His ability to question Peter on an issue like the relation to the Gentiles, such as we discussed in question 11, should not be seen as a challenge to universal authority. Paul comes across in his letters in an authoritative manner. He defends his own apostleship as valid in relation to the other apostles. Thus his willingness to challenge Peter or the other key figures in the Jerusalem church (James the brother of the Lord) grew out of his own understanding of the call he received from Jesus Christ.

27. Why does Paul come across as if he alone has the truth? Didn't he bully others into accepting his opinions?

I am not sure if you have specific passages from Paul in mind or not. I understand how one can get the impression that Paul is quite strong in his positions. Perhaps his strongest letter is Galatians. He makes some very negative comments about those who are disrupting the Galatian community. You may notice that right at the beginning of Galatians Paul launches into an argumentative attack on those who have deserted his preached message so quickly (Gal 1:6–9). He strongly rejects the opinion of those who are sowing seeds of dissension among the Galatians, insisting that circumcision still be practiced. So upset does Paul become that he even says, "I wish those who unsettle you would castrate themselves!" (Gal 5:12). I would classify Paul as a strongly opinionated person, but I would not consider him a bully. I will admit that I might find it difficult to live with him (as with many of the saints), but I do not think Paul is rigid. Rather, he is a man of firm conviction. In almost all of his letters Paul writes forcefully and with great resolve. He feels that the gospel message he has received and that he carries forth has its uncompromising aspects that all believers should acknowledge. Because his message is not of human origin but from God, there can be no waffling on essential matters of faith. You might say that Paul is the perfect example of a "convert" who goes all the way and never wants to look back. He believes his former life has been surpassed by what he has gained from Jesus Christ (Phil 3:8). That is why he is so firm in much of what he has to say.

Moreover, there are passages in Paul where his tender side comes through. He treats his congregations like good parents treat their children. He says to the Corinthians, "I fed you with milk, not solid food, for you were not ready for solid food" (1 Cor 3:2). He sometimes addresses his communities as "children" (1 Cor 4:14; 2 Cor 6:13; Gal 4:19). At first glance, this might appear condescending. It expresses rather Paul's familial tendency to view the Christian community as a family. He is the father; they are his children. He even compares himself to a nursing mother caring for her infants (1 Thess 2:7–8). Sometimes he admonishes them sternly and disciplines them. At other times he tries to persuade and exhort. (See 1 Thess 4:18–5:11 where Paul uses the same Greek verb *[parakaleō]* to alternate between consolation and exhortation.) In fact, the tone of most of the ethical sections of his letters is not one of bullying people to accept the truth but trying persuasively to present it so that they will be convinced of it.

28. How can Paul say he wants to be "all things to all people"? Isn't that unhealthy?

From a modern psychological point of view, it is. But we need to place Paul's words in context to understand them properly. The passage you are referring to is in First Corinthians. Paul says, "I have become all things to all people, that I might by all means save some. I do it all for the sake of the gospel, so that I may share in its blessings" (1 Cor 9:22–23). These famous words conclude a short section in which Paul describes the paradox of the freedom he has as an apostle. Within 1 Corinthians 9 Paul offers different examples that express his general sentiment:

1. To the Jews I became as a Jew, in order to win Jews (v. 20).
2. To those outside the law I became as one outside the law…so that I might win those outside the law (v. 21).
3. To the weak I became weak, so that I might win the weak (v. 22).

These sentences encompass all the possibilities Paul has dealt with in the Corinthian community, Jews, Gentiles, and those who are "weak" in the sense that their faith is underdeveloped. Paul does not try to win them over for his own benefit. That is, he is not trying to win "brownie points" with people so that they will accept him. His willingness to be adaptable to the situation is strictly for their salvation in Jesus Christ (1 Cor 10:33). Note that the first two phrases contain the word "as." Paul functions as a Jew and as a Gentile so as to be effective in proclaiming his message to them. This perspective was particularly important for the Corinthians to grasp. Theirs was a community with many divisions in which people had become intolerant of one another. Paul is indicating that, paradoxically, Christian freedom embraces giving up that which we might prefer so that a greater good might come of it. He began the passage we've just looked at with these words: "For though I am free with respect to all, I have made myself a slave to all, so that I might win more of them" (1 Cor 9:19). Thus he is not speaking psychologically or politically about changing positions simply to please others. He is speaking of the dramatic freedom that has come to him in Christ Jesus and enables him to appeal to a broad spectrum of people.

29. I've heard people say that Paul was anti-Semitic. Is this true?

First, I would not use the term "anti-Semitic" with regard to any NT material, since the term is a modern one that describes actions and attitudes that do not pertain explicitly to ancient times. Yet one can legitimately ask if Paul is "anti-Jewish." My response is, no, I do not believe he is. But there are problematic passages in the Pauline letters that have to be approached cautiously. The most blatant passage is in First Thessalonians, which speaks of the "Jews, who killed both the Lord Jesus and the prophets and drove us out..." (1 Thess 2:15). It goes so far as to say that "God's wrath has overtaken them at last" (1 Thess 2:16). First, I should point out that some scholars think this passage is not genuinely from Paul. They believe a later author wrote it. In the course of the transmission of Paul's letters, it was inserted into this genuinely Pauline letter and thus came to represent Paul's perspective. That may be, but it would still not affect the fact that the passage is found in a canonical book and has been improperly used in history to justify anti-Jewish attitudes or behaviors.

Second, Paul himself was a Jew (and thus a Semite). Even after his commission from the risen Lord to go to the Gentiles he does not disavow his Jewishness. He remained a Jew, albeit one who believed that Jesus was the messiah and God's Son. Indeed at times he proudly recalls his Jewish heritage and invokes it as part of his apostolic call (Rom 11:1; 2 Cor 11:22; Phil 3:5–6). Paul phrases these passages in the present tense. His understanding of what the Jewish requisites of the law now demand of him as a follower of Jesus has changed, but his Jewish identity has not. Consequently, I prefer to see Paul's words regarding his Jewish colleagues as part of the first-century discussion about theological disagreements that Jews often held among themselves. Paul is not anti-Jewish in such instances. He simply takes positions that some Jews took in opposition to others who viewed life differently. The Qumran community is another example of intra-Jewish bickering. These Jews left Jerusalem and went down to the Dead Sea to preserve a form of Judaism that they felt was more authentic than the adapted Judaism in the city.

A third aspect of this question is Paul's complex understanding of the role of Israel in salvation history. This issue demands separate treatment (see question 76), but a few words are in order here. Romans 9—11 most systematically lays out Paul's outlook on Israel. There Paul asserts that God has not abandoned his people (Rom 9:1–2) and that ultimately Israel will be saved along with the Gentiles (Rom 11:26; cf. 10:1 where Paul expresses his wish for this salvation). So how does one interpret the view that some Jews were involved in the demise of Jesus?

I believe that in 1 Thessalonians 2:15 Paul is speaking of a small group of Jews from Jerusalem who were involved in plotting against Jesus. He is not speaking of Jews for all time. Moreover, Paul understands this action to be a sad part of the history of God's chosen people. From his historical overview, Israel regularly rejected prophetic figures God sent to the people (cf. Matt 5:11–12; 23:37). What happened to Jesus followed this unfortunate history, as did the persecutions that dogged Paul and his companions. He goes on to interpret these sufferings as an essential element of the gospel of Jesus Christ. That is why Christians themselves are marked with the sign of the cross (1 Cor 1:18). Finally, the notion of the "wrath of God" in Paul is not restricted to those Jews who partook of the plot against Jesus. God's wrath is what Paul believes comes upon all sinners, Jew or Gentile, who do not conform to God's will in their lives (Rom 13:4).

THREE

THE COMMUNITIES AND COMPANIONS OF PAUL

30. How many journeys did Paul make? Was he the only missionary to travel so widely?

According to Acts Paul made three missionary journeys and a final journey to Rome to face charges against him. I will use a chart to summarize these journeys. Please refer to the maps in the Appendix.

Paul's Journeys in Acts	Description
1st Journey: Acts Acts 13:1—14:28	Barnabas and Paul sail from Antioch (Syria) to Cyprus, then from Paphos to Perga in Pamphilia and on to Antioch in Pisidia and Iconium, Lystra, and Derbe in Asia Minor.
Council of Jerusalem: Act 15:1–35 (Interim)	Paul goes to Jerusalem in the intervening time and eventually returns with Barnabas to Antioch (Syria) with approval to go to the Gentiles.
2nd Journey: Acts 15:36—18:22	After a sharp disagreement with Barnabas, Paul chooses Silas (Silvanus) as his companion to evangelize throughout Syria and Cilicia, his home province in Asia Minor, as well as Phrygia and Galatia. At Troas on the coast of Asia

2nd Journey (cont'd)	Minor, Paul has a vision that sends him by boat to Macedonia, on the European continent. He proceeds on land to Philippi, Thessalonica, Beroea, Athens, and Corinth. He then sails to Ephesus in Asia Minor and onto Caesarea and Jerusalem, finally returning to Antioch (Syria).
3rd Journey: Acts 18:23—21:17	From Jerusalem Paul goes back to Galatia, Phrygia, and Ephesus, finally crossing over again to Macedonia. Originally intending to sail back to Syria, he is forced by a plot against him to return through Macedonia to Troas. Then by sea he and his companions go to Mytilene, Samos, and Miletus, sailing past Ephesus to go to Rhodes and then to Tyre in Syria. After a short time he returns to Jerusalem to meet with James.
4th Journey: Acts 27:1—28:16	After appearing before Festus and Agrippa in Caesarea, Paul is sent to Rome with other prisoners. From Caesarea they sail to Sidon, to Myra, a city in Licia in Asia Minor, and then

4th Journey (cont'd)	to Crete, where weather problems hamper the voyage severely. They are shipwrecked on Malta, and after three months, sail on to Syracuse, Rhegium, and Rome, where Paul remains under house arrest.

You can see by this outline that Paul's travels were quite extensive. One scholar has calculated the extent of Paul's missionary journeys as covering some 10,000 miles. Paul himself mentions his travels in Second Corinthians, where he speaks of frequent journeys and several shipwrecks (2 Cor 11:25–26). He used both land and sea routes, although sailing was restricted to certain times of the year when the weather was not a serious threat (see Acts 28:11, which mentions a ship that "wintered" on an island). The road system of the Roman Empire enabled a convenient transportation network. One major road frequented by Paul was the Via Egnatia that ran from west to east. Along it lay cities like Thessalonica and Philippi that Paul visited.

This outline of three missionary journeys is plausible. Yet we should remember two qualifiers to this statement: (1) it cannot be reconstructed from Paul's letters in this fashion; (2) many ancient writings used the motif of the *journey* to tell the stories of their heroes. Acts has many details to describe situations in some of Paul's churches, such as Corinth, Philippi, and Ephesus. Yet we cannot know for certain that Paul made only three major missionary journeys. He may well have taken other trips. Some of his time is unaccounted for, especially the time in Arabia (Gal 1:17).

There is also a question of how to date the fourteen years between his visits to Jerusalem, which he mentions at the beginning of his own ministry (Gal 2:1). Does this mean fourteen years from the time of his conversion or from the time of his first visit to Jerusalem? The Letter to the Galatians contains the most extensive account of Paul's travels (Gal 1:17–2:1). It broadly indicates that after his conversion he went to Arabia (perhaps Nabatea), after which he returned to Damascus. Then after three years he went to Jerusalem for the first time, followed by journeys to Syria and his home province of Cilicia. Paul then describes how he went to Jerusalem after fourteen years for the Jerusalem Council. Some of this clearly coincides with the Acts outline above; some of it is more elusive. What is certain is that Paul saw himself as an itinerant missionary whose primary call as apostle to the Gentiles required extensive travel throughout the Roman Empire. Indeed, his plan was apparently a steady expansion westward toward Spain and the outer reaches of the empire (see Rom 15:24, 28).

He was not the sole missionary to travel extensively. Though Paul's preference was to go to new, unevangelized apostolic fields (see Rom 15:20–21), he sometimes visited places where the gospel had already spread before his arrival. In such instances, he admits, "…I was still unknown by sight to the churches of Judea that are in Christ; they only heard it said, 'The one who formerly was persecuting us is now proclaiming the faith he once tried to destroy.' And they glorified God because of me" (Gal 1:21–24). History does not record the names of many of these early missionaries. Some are known by ancient traditions that cannot always be verified, others remain totally unknown. Peter, for instance, presumably ministered in Rome, but Paul's Letter to the Romans gives no acknowledgment of this tradition. Paul also had companions who sometimes went on missions of their own.

In short, the early church grew largely because of itinerant missionaries like Paul who were willing to take the great risks that accompanied any journey (2 Cor 11:26). As Paul indicates, he experienced some of these, including shipwreck, bandits and pirates, hard work, hunger and thirst, lack of shelter, and so on (2 Cor 11:25–28). Traveling was not easy in Paul's day. Most people traveled on foot. Merchants had pack animals and carts, but only the military or government used horses for transportation. Travel on ships was not by luxury liner. Normally, travelers booked passage on merchant ships heading in their direction (as in Acts 21:2–3; 27:2). Despite the obstacles, missionaries like Paul spread the gospel message with incredible efficiency.

31. Was there a plan to Paul's journeys?

Paul's journeys were not haphazard. His move from Judea toward the western part of the empire was a natural one because Rome was the center of the empire. Christianity originally sprang up in Jerusalem but quickly spread to other parts of the Greco-Roman world. Acts envisions this process as a geographical advance accomplished under the guidance of the Holy Spirit. In an important programmatic passage in Acts the risen Lord says to his apostles, "…you will receive power when the Holy Spirit has come upon you; and you will be my witnesses in Jerusalem, in all Judea and Samaria, and to the ends of the earth" (Acts 1:8). This presents an idealized picture of how Christianity spread, but it is followed in the general outline of Acts. This growth is part of God's divine plan. The church prospers under the guidance of the Holy Spirit and Christianity moves out into the Gentile world, with Paul being the primary figure to promote its success.

Even granting the tendency of Acts to idealize the picture of life in the early church, this outline conforms to Paul's own view of how his ministry developed. He praises God in his ministry "according to the revelation of the mystery that was kept secret for long ages" (Rom 16:25). For Paul, the mystery is God's plan for salvation that in Jesus Christ is now coming to fruition in the new life of faith seen in the church. Thus his evangelization of the Gentile world takes place in accord with God's plan. Apostles are "stewards of God's mysteries" (1 Cor 4:1) who are compelled by their faith to go forth and carry the good news of Jesus Christ to Jew and Gentile alike so that all might be saved (Rom 11:32).

Paul is adamant in saying that his plans are not simply his own but come from God (2 Cor 1:17–22). In his letters Paul often expresses the intention of going to visit the various communities that he founded (1 Cor 16:5; 2 Cor 1:15–16; 13:2). Once he even mentions wanting to avoid a visitation to the Corinthians because it might cause too much emotional strain (2 Cor 2:1). Sometimes he also speaks for the intentions of his colleagues:

> If Timothy comes, see that he has nothing to fear among you, for he is doing the work of the Lord just as I am; therefore let no one despise him. Send him on his way in peace, so that he may come to me; for I am expecting him with the brothers. Now concerning our brother Apollos, I strongly urged him to visit you with the other brothers, but he was not at all willing to come now. He will come when he has the opportunity. (1 Cor 16:10–12)

He also expresses the intention to cast his gospel nets very wide, as when he tells the Romans he intends to go to Spain after spending time getting acquainted with them (Rom 15:24, 28).

If all of this sounds mundane, it is not. Paul sees the necessity of making plans in his ministry as an expression of the fulfillment of God's intentions regarding the spread of the gospel message.

32. You sometimes use the word "community" and sometimes "church." What does Paul mean by the word "church"?

First let's clarify what Paul does not mean. He is not speaking of a building. Nor does "church" mean the universal church as we have come to know it, although this concept is developed in the later Deutero-Pauline letters (Eph 5:25–27, 32; Col 1:24) and has roots in Paul's notion. Paul primarily understands the church as a local community of baptized followers of Jesus Christ. This understanding is not due to Paul's opposition to the idea of a universal church. Rather, in his day the local congregation was central to his experience. Everywhere Paul went he either founded local communities of Christians or visited already established communities. The Greek word *ekklēsia* (whence our word "ecclesiastical"), which appears in the Pauline letters more than sixty times, means "those who are called" or an "assembly" of the people of God. In secular terms, it described an assembly of free citizens. This term also has a Jewish background. Judaism saw itself as the assembly *(qahal)* of God. It is thus possible to interchange the word "community" with the word "church" for purposes of variation, but Paul has a profound understanding of church. It always refers to God's chosen community.

Paul can use the term in a variety of contexts. He speaks of the "church of God" either in the sense of the local faith community of a given town (1 Cor 1:2; 2 Cor 1:1) or in a more general sense of the group of believers whom he had previously persecuted (1 Cor 15:9; Gal 1:13). The latter usage already leans toward the later universal sense of church that develops in the Deutero-Pauline letters. The plural expression "churches of God" (1 Cor 11:16; 1 Thess 2:14) indicates how Paul still views the Christian communities from an individual angle even while asserting the interrelationship between them as a fellowship. When Paul speaks of churches (plural) he often is referring to diverse communities within a geographic region. He specifically mentions the churches of Galatia (1 Cor 16:1; Gal 1:2), of Macedonia (2 Cor 8:1), of Asia (1 Cor 16:19), and of Judea (Gal 1:22).

Paul's understanding of the significance of these communities goes beyond the word "church." His favorite term for the members of the churches is the community of "saints" (Rom 1:7; 15:26; 1 Cor 1:2; etc.). The idea of Christians being the "holy ones" probably antedates Paul, but he uses the term with great frequency and conviction. The church is a community called by God to be holy, set apart for the sacred duty of spreading the good news of salvation, and consecrated for service. Paul does not naively think that the saints are perfect. Their holiness is derivative of God. God has called them; God makes them holy. Note that the term only occurs in the plural in Paul's letters. Being a "saint" is not a matter of personal holiness but of membership in the community called "church." God has sanctified the church to become a community of righteous believers whose human limitations no longer hold sway in life (Rom 6:19–22).

Even more impressive is another image that Paul uses of the church. The Corinthian letters contain the most references to the church. Corinth was a community filled with divisions that Paul tried to unify. Not surprisingly, Paul's most important image for church comes from the Corinthian correspondence, namely, the church as the "body of Christ." The phrase is found only four times in the Pauline letters (Rom 7:4; 1 Cor 10:16; 12:27; Eph 4:12; the first two references do not specifically refer to the "church" but to Christ) but there can be no doubt that it is Paul's single most important ecclesial image. Paul speaks eloquently of the church as the body of Christ in the famous passage 1 Corinthians 12:1–31. He uses the analogy of the human body to illustrate the miraculous diversity and unity that derives from the risen Lord Jesus who has invited the church to become his body. The entire passage is worthy of lengthy reflection, but I quote only two important lines:

> For just as the body is one and has many members, and all the members of the body, though many, are one body, so it is with Christ....Now you are the body of Christ and individually members of it. (1 Cor 12:12, 27)

The background for the notion of the church as the body of Christ is found in Greek society. Greeks had great admiration for the human body, and the body became a prominent metaphor for a unified whole. Each part of the body has a role to play in the healthy functioning of the whole body. Paul carries the notion further than the secular background implies by insisting that we are baptized into Christ (Rom 6:3) and thereby become a part of the body of Christ. Each member of the body of Christ possesses the dignity of the body. Each member has his or her own gifts and duties. But all must exercise these gifts for building up the body of

Christ. At Corinth Paul sharply reprimanded his readers for their divisions. The Eucharist both called them to be and shaped them into a unified whole. He called them back to the unity of the body of Christ. They were called to be a eucharistic community united around the table of the Lord precisely because they were the body of Christ. In this image he has left a lasting legacy in the Church.

33. Can you describe what Paul's churches were like? What is a "house church"? How many people belonged?

That is difficult to say with any precision. Unfortunately Paul does not speak explicitly of numbers in the communities he founded or visited. Numerical information must be deduced from reading between the lines and from archaeological data. I will address this issue in a moment. But first let's turn to the question of location.

In the previous question I pointed out that Paul did not use the word "church" to describe a building. So where did Paul's communities gather as church? Probably in two places initially. Since many of the early communities had Jewish adherents, at first they would gather together with other pious Jews in the local synagogue for readings and prayer. Then they would gather in people's private homes to celebrate the Lord's Supper. First Corinthians provides a picture of such a eucharistic gathering in the section where Paul reprimands their rude behavior (1 Cor 11:17–22). Acts illustrates a similar procedure (Acts 18:7–8) and frequently indicates that Paul went to synagogues to preach the Word of God (Acts 14:1; 17:1–2). Interestingly, Paul never uses the word "synagogue" in his own letters. Christianity in Paul's day had no meeting place comparable to the Jewish synagogue. Instead Paul's letters indicate that early believers met in what scholars call "house churches." These were private homes of wealthy individuals who had the space, the means, and the inclination to host gatherings of the faithful. Paul mentions such persons in relation to the church in Corinth. In the Letter to the

Romans, Paul sends greetings from "Gaius, who is host to me and to the whole church..." (Rom 16:23; cf. 16:3–5). In First Corinthians he sends greetings from "Aquila and Prisca, together with the church in their house..." (1 Cor 16:19; cf. Phlm 2). Archaeology in Corinth has yielded some homes from the Roman period that give some idea of the size and shape of such house churches. On this basis one scholar has estimated the size of a house church in Corinth to be no more than 50–60 people, and that would make a crowded fit in most Roman-style villas. Other scholars think large villas could have held considerably more people when you take into account all the rooms available. In large cities, early Christians could also have met in small apartments (*insulae*) for their rituals. Apparently in Corinth a controversy existed over the way the community would gather to celebrate the Eucharist in a house church (1 Cor 11:17–34). Paul describes the situation thus:

> When you come together, it is not really to eat the Lord's supper. For when the time comes to eat, each of you goes ahead with your own supper, and one goes hungry and another becomes drunk. What! Do you not have homes to eat and drink in? Or do you show contempt for the church of God and humiliate those who have nothing? What should I say to you? Should I commend you? In this matter I do not commend you! (1 Cor 11:20–22)

Perhaps the crowded conditions led to a divided practice whereby the elite members of the community proceeded with their supper in the dining room, while the lower classes waited for their turn. The Roman practice of dining was done reclining on couches (see Luke 11:37 NAB), a practice that inevitably took up quite a bit of space in the dining room. We do not know the actual circumstances that prompted Paul's response, but we can surmise that house churches constituted rather small gatherings in private homes.

34. Paul mentions companions who accompanied him on his missionary journeys. Can you say more about them?

We know the names of many of Paul's companions and coworkers but often detailed information on their lives and background is lacking. I will begin with the most prominent companions, Timothy, Titus, Silvanus, Barnabas, and Apollos.

Timothy and Titus are justifiably among the most prominent because of the letters addressed to them. Even if those letters are deemed not to be from Paul himself, these figures were genuinely companions of Paul known from his own letters and Acts. Timothy is explicitly called a "co-worker" (Rom 16:21), and Paul uses tender words to describe him as "my beloved and faithful child" (1 Cor 4:17) whose "worth you know, how like a son with a father he has served with me in the work of the gospel" (Phil 2:22). Paul also lists Timothy as a co-sender of some of his letters (2 Cor 1:1; Phlm 1:1), at least in the sense that Timothy shares Paul's thoughts as well as his ministry. Timothy was already a convert in Lystra, Asia Minor, when he met Paul. He was the child of a Jewish mother and a Gentile father whom Paul had circumcised in order not to scandalize the Jewish Christians who still held to the practice of circumcision (Acts 16:1–3).

Unlike Timothy, Titus is never mentioned in Acts. Only Paul's letters speak of this companion. Titus was a Gentile Christian whom Paul calls "my brother" (2 Cor 2:13) and "my partner *(koinonos)* and co-worker *(synergos)*" (2 Cor 8:23). His main service to Paul was serving as a courier to the Corinthian community with whom Titus had a strong relationship (2 Cor 7:13–14). He also helped Paul collect money from the Corinthians for the support of the Jerusalem church (2 Cor 8:1–7). Paul describes an important incident in an autobiographical section of Galatians when he says that, although he was Greek, Titus was never compelled to be circumcised when Paul confronted the Jerusalem leaders about the implications of the mission to the Gentiles (Gal 2:1–3). In essence, Paul uses Titus as a type of test case in Galatians for his understanding that followers of Jesus

Christ should no longer practice circumcision for religious purposes.

Silvanus, the Latin form of the Greek name Silas, was one of the "prophets" in the Jerusalem church (Acts 15:32). The early Christian community thought of prophets as mouthpieces of God whose gift was to help discern God's will. A companion on several missionary ventures, Paul lists Silvanus as a co-sender to the Thessalonians (1 Thess 1:1; 2 Thess 1:1). He assisted Paul with the evangelization of Corinth (2 Cor 1:19). As a Jewish Christian, Silas became a trusted companion with Paul in the mission to the Gentiles. Paul eventually chose him to replace Barnabas to accompany him on his journeys (Acts 15:36–40).

Barnabas, a Jewish Levite, figures prominently in the Letter to the Galatians (Gal 2:1–13; cf. also 1 Cor 9:6). Paul says that he was involved in a controversy, insisting that the Gentiles conform to the traditional Jewish dietary regulations. Originally Barnabas accompanied Paul to Jerusalem and received the blessing to go to the Gentiles. But Paul says that Barnabas later reneged and "was led away by their hypocrisy" (Gal 2:13). One should note that Barnabas brought Paul to Antioch (Acts 11:25) and made Paul his coworker (cf. Acts 14:2). Acts indicates that Paul and Barnabas had a falling out over a certain John Mark whom Paul did not want on his next mission because of his backing out of an earlier missionary effort, but whom Barnabas wanted as a companion (Acts 15:37). John Mark was probably a relative of Barnabas, for Colossians refers to a "Mark the cousin of Barnabas." The result was that Barnabas went his own way with Mark and Paul chose Silas to go another direction (Acts 15:39–40).

Another rather well-known companion of Paul was Apollos. Mentioned in both Acts and First Corinthians, Apollos was a native of Alexandria, Egypt, another diaspora Jew who ministered in Ephesus and then in Corinth (Acts 18:24–28). The Corinthians obviously admired him, so much so that some saw themselves as the Apollos party (1 Cor 1:12). Paul worked against this kind of over-identification with a specific minister, although

Paul nowhere indicates that Apollos himself fostered such an attitude. Paul places any competitive temptation in ministry in perspective: "I planted, Apollos watered, but God gave the growth" (1 Cor 3:6). In addition to these more famous companions is a host of others. Some are only names about whom we know little. The concluding chapter in Romans, for instance, lists a large number of names in Paul's greetings (Rom 16:3–23). This seems unusual when writing to a community that Paul did not found. Yet it is indicative of the large number of colleagues, coworkers, and acquaintances Paul had. Paul lists as coworkers Urbanus (Rom 16:9), Epaphroditus from Philippi (Phil 2:25), Clement (Phil 4:3), and Philemon (Phlm 1), as well as Mark, Demas, Aristarchus, and Luke (Phlm 24). He also mentions Epaphras who ministered to the church at Colossae (Col 1:7; 4:12). Paul also lists one prominent married couple as colleagues, Aquila and Prisca (Rom 16:3). They hailed from Rome, whence they came to Corinth at the time the Emperor Claudius issued his decree expelling the Jews from the city (ca. A.D. 44, Acts 18:2). Paul worked with them in the same trade of "tentmaking" in Corinth and later in Ephesus. They maintained a house church (1 Cor 16:19). Women's names also appear frequently as important members of Paul's communities such as Chloe, Lydia, Nympha, Tryphaena, Tryphosa, and others.

My detailed response to your questions is indicative of a number of important observations. First, Paul was not a loner in ministry. At times he followed upon the footsteps of predecessors who had evangelized in areas he visited. At other times he enlisted many colleagues and coworkers. Sometimes they suffered along with him for the sake of their ministry. He became quite attached to many of them, and some of them were his most trusted means of communication between himself and his churches. Second, we can note with some satisfaction that all was not perfect in the early church. Paul obviously had some sharp disagreements with some of his close colleagues, even to the point of an irreconcilable split. Cooperative ministry was difficult in Paul's day, too.

35. Can you explain more about the women you have mentioned? Did they have special roles in his churches?

Yes, some of the women in Paul's churches had special roles, but it is difficult to describe them precisely. The previous question mentioned in passing some women in Paul's churches, but your question allows me to explain this item in more depth. (See also Florence Gillman's book in the Recommended Readings.)

Chloe was a woman in Corinth whose "people" sent word to Paul about the bickering in the Corinthian church (1 Cor 1:11). She possesses no title or description, but the mention of her "people" makes it likely that she was a business woman or perhaps head of a household. Paul never mentions Lydia in his own letters, but Acts indicates that she was among the first Christian converts in Philippi (Acts 16:15). Acts portrays Lydia as "a dealer in purple cloth" who was head of her own household (Acts 16:14). This portrait makes her a fairly wealthy businesswoman, probably a woman of means and influence in the Philippian community. We have already mentioned the married couple Aquila and Prisca (whom Acts always names Priscilla). They worked with Paul intimately at Corinth in their mutual work of tentmaking (Acts 18:2–3). Not only does Paul mention their house church, but he also commends them as "my co-workers in Christ Jesus, who risked their necks for my life" (Rom 16:3–4 NAB). One cannot know the division of labor of such a couple, but nowhere is Aquila mentioned without his wife, Prisca. Possibly the fact that Priscilla's name is often mentioned first indicates that she was the more prominent member of the team (Rom 16:3; Acts 18:18). They were a team with Paul in ministry.

The Letter to the Philippians recalls two other female coworkers with Paul, Euodia and Syntyche. Paul includes these women among those who "have struggled beside me in the work of the gospel, together with Clement and the rest of my co-workers, whose names are in the book of life" (Phil 4:3). But Paul expresses concern about some sort of disagreement that has arisen between these two women. He urges them "to be of the same mind in the Lord" (Phil 4:2). What was their specific role in Philippi? What was the nature of their disagreement? Paul does not say.

Among the many references to people in Romans (Rom 16:3–23), Paul commends a woman named Mary who "has worked very hard among you" (Rom 16:6). The nature of her work, however, is never clarified. In the same list of greetings Paul singles out Julia and the sister of Nereus (Rom 16:15) as worthy of mention, but again he leaves out any specifics as to their role in the community. Paul places upon one woman in the list in Romans a title of some significance. Paul calls Phoebe a "deacon *(diakonos)* of the church at Cenchreae" (Rom 16:1). Clearly Paul had female coworkers, some of whom held significant positions in his various communities. In fact, I don't believe it is farfetched to say that Paul offers contemporary ministers a model of cooperative ministry.

36. Was Phoebe an *ordained* deacon?

Your question does not permit a quick response. Let me first quote the complete passage that names Phoebe.

> I commend to you our sister *(adelphē)* Phoebe, a deacon *(diakonos)* of the church at Cenchreae, so that you may welcome her in the Lord as is fitting for the saints, and help her in whatever she may require from you, for she has been a benefactor *(prostatis)* of many and of myself as well. (Rom 16:1–2)

Phoebe is a coworker of Paul who apparently is carrying to Rome the letter Paul has written for the Romans. She needs hospitality during her visit. Paul commends her for what she has done for the Corinthian church as well as for himself. She ministered as a "deacon" in Cenchreae, a town next to Corinth on the Isthmian peninsula. The town had an important seaport that allowed access to the Aegean Sea in the east. It held a prominent Christian community, and Phoebe was probably a native of this area.

Now note that Paul attributes three titles to Phoebe: a sister, a deacon, and a benefactor. The first term is a standard familial term used metaphorically. Paul's communities regularly referred to one another as "brother" and "sister" because they were the family of God. The second is the masculine form of a formal ministry of service. But it would be anachronistic to speak of this ministry as an "ordained" ministry. Ordination as we understand it was a much later development in the life of the church. At this time, there were distinctive ministries that eventually evolved into specified, ordained ministries. The word "deacon" means some sort of formal service in the community. Paul calls others "deacons," such as Apollos and himself (1 Cor 3:5). This diaconal ministry implies preaching the Word of God and working to build up the Christian community. There is no reason to suspect that Paul means anything more or less when he applies the term "deacon" to Phoebe. The third term, which can also be translated "patron," occurs nowhere else in the NT. It could have the connotation of being a legal patroness, that is, a sponsor, but it may also simply mean that she had the financial means to support Paul's ministry and perhaps the Corinthian church. Whatever the exact nature of her functions in Cenchreae, she was doubtless a leader in the Christian community. Paul has no hesitation to commend her in that role.

37. Who became the leaders of Paul's churches when he left them?

What you are really asking is the kind of leadership structure that Paul left in his churches. Frankly, we do not know who functioned as leaders and in what capacity once Paul moved on to a new geographical region for ministry. Paul's churches seem to have been more charismatic in orientation. This meant that leadership emerged from talented people within the community. Paul's Corinthian correspondence lends a tantalizing view of a community with regard to ministry. To say that Paul's churches were more charismatic in orientation is not to say that they were entirely egalitarian. You will remember how strongly Paul reminded the Corinthians: "For in the one Spirit we were all baptized into one body—Jews or Greeks, slaves or free—and we were all made to drink of one Spirit" (1 Cor 12:13). Paul was against elitism that broke down into factions. Yet Paul goes on in the same chapter to delineate distinctive roles within the Christian community.

> Now you are the body of Christ and individually members of it. And God has appointed in the church first apostles, second prophets, third teachers; then deeds of power, then gifts of healing, forms of assistance, forms of leadership, various kinds of tongues. Are all apostles? Are all prophets? Are all teachers? Do all work miracles? Do all possess gifts of healing? Do all speak in tongues? Do all interpret? But strive for the greater gifts. (1 Cor 12:27–31)

There is a hierarchy in this listing. Paul conceives of apostleship as a primary ministerial role in the community. This apostleship derives not from simply having known Jesus of Nazareth but from having been called by the risen Lord. Unfortunately, Paul never explicitly says who played what role within his communities once he went on the road. (But see the mention of "overseers and ministers" in Philippians 1:1.) There were others in the communities, such as prophets and teachers, who exercised important roles (e.g., 1 Cor 12:28–29). Clearly, coworkers like Timothy or Titus were key figures in maintaining contact. At the same time, Paul seems to allow whatever local structure that had evolved in the local church to continue functioning unless a serious problem arose. At Corinth, for instance, factionalism was destroying the very fabric of the community, so Paul strongly encourages them to avoid dividing into groups to follow one specific leader or another (1 Cor 3:1–9).

In the Pastoral Epistles, which likely postdate Paul, we finally see the developing character of community leadership that shaped the later Church. Passing on authority by "laying on of hands" (1 Tim 4:14; 2 Tim 1:6) and exhorting these ministers to exercise their authority responsibly becomes a major concern. Eventually, further distinctive roles emerged (*episkopoi* = overseers, supervisors; *presbyteroi* = elders, presbyters; *diakonoi* = ministers, assistants) that met the needs of the growing church. These may have paralleled somewhat positions in the Jewish synagogue and can be seen as antecedents of modern church ministries. While some scholars (and certain Christian communions) judge these developments to be aberrations that distorted Paul's vision, others would classify them as legitimate and logical developments under the guidance of the Holy Spirit.

Four

Paul's Letters

38. Why did Paul write letters? Why didn't he write a Gospel?

I will take the second part of your question first. No one knows why Paul did not write a Gospel. Keep in mind that all four Gospels in our NT date between three and thirty-five years after the death of Paul. The following chart gives a sense of the span of dates in the NT.

Date A.D.	NT Document
51–63/64	Paul's letters
66–70	Gospel of Mark
80–90	Gospel of Matthew Gospel of Luke
90–100	Gospel of John
100–110	Last NT documents (e.g., 2 Peter)

None of the Gospels originated in a Pauline church. According to the best research to date, Gospels did not exist prior to Christianity. No type of literature found in the ancient Jewish or Greco-Roman world exactly conforms to our canonical Gospels. The Gospels clearly focus on the life, ministry, death, and resurrection of Jesus of Nazareth. Paul displays little interest in presenting such a narrative and seemingly historical understanding of Jesus. Paul says very little about the "story" of Jesus of Nazareth apart from his death and resurrection. Instead, he wrote letters.

Why does anyone write a letter? A letter is an act of communication. Paul had gone throughout the Mediterranean world establishing faith communities and building relationships with their members. Because Paul viewed his own ministry as an itinerant one that always required him to move on to the next town or region, he needed to have a way of maintaining contact with the communities that he left behind. Letters afforded him that opportunity. In essence, they might be considered a continuation and extension of his apostolic, pastoral ministry.

In Paul's world, letter writing was a well-established art. People regularly dictated letters to be sent to family members, friends, relatives, business partners, and so on. One ancient source reveals that at least twenty-one different forms of letters were known in the Greco-Roman world. Demetrius of Phalerum categorizes the rhetorical forms of letters as friendly, commendatory, advisory, apologetic, thankful, admonishing, and so on. I think Paul wrote letters to stay in touch with his congregations and his coworkers and to offer them corrections, commendations, and advice. At times he also wrote letters to introduce himself to a community that he did not found, such as the Letter to the Romans.

It is also interesting to note that twenty-one of the twenty-seven books of the NT are in letter form. In addition, the Book of Revelation includes letters (Rev 1:4—3:22), even though the form of the book is not a letter. The letter is represented more predominantly in the Christian scriptures than any other literary form. Paul is the one who introduced it into the Christian mindset, for his letters are the oldest written material in the NT. This is all the more significant when one considers that no book of the OT is in the form of a letter, even though the OT sometimes refers to letters (2 Sam 11:14–15; 2 Kgs 5:5–7; Ezra 4:7–18). My point is that letter writing was obviously an important form of communication in the early church. Paul remains our best example of it.

39. Why would Paul dictate his letters if he knew how to read and write? How did he circulate his letters?

Dictation of letters was the standard practice in Paul's day. Most people were uneducated formally and thus could neither read nor write, at least with any facility. Whenever individuals wanted to write a letter, they would go to a professionally trained scribe (technically called by scholars an *amanuensis* [= one who writes by hand]) and pay a fee to have the scribe write a letter that the client dictated. One can see evidence of the use of a scribe in Romans 16:22. In the last paragraphs of this chapter comes a greeting from a different person who apparently was Paul's scribe at the time: "I Tertius, the writer of this letter, greet you in the Lord." Nothing else is known of this Tertius but the reference is to be understood literally that he *wrote* the letter with the implication that Paul dictated. Nowhere else in Paul's letters is there mention of other scribes.

It is possible that some of Paul's named colleagues, such as Timothy or Silvanus, occasionally functioned as scribes, but generally scribes remain the anonymous writers in the background. In other places we can infer that Paul usually used scribes because Paul sometimes makes reference to his own written insertions into the letters, as in First Corinthians: "I, Paul, write this greeting with my own hand" (1 Cor 16:21; see also Gal 6:11; Col 4:18; 2 Thess 3:17; Phlm 19). One might question what effect such an insertion is meant to convey to the readers of the letter. Does it perhaps lend more authority to the letter that the "author" takes the time to write something in his own hand? Or does it convey more a sense of familiarity and friendliness? In the case of Paul's letters, it might be both.

Concerning the second part of your question, Paul used the standard means of circulating letters in his day. Since only government officials and the military could use the formal mail system of the Roman Empire, whereby mail was delivered by chariot-riding mail carriers, the common people had to use trusted slaves or companions to deliver letters, messages, and parcels.

Paul, in fact, refers to sending trusted companions like Timothy and Titus to various communities with messages (1 Thess 3:2; 2 Cor 12:18). They, in turn, brought him oral reports or written correspondence from the communities. This was the most common way for Paul to send and receive his correspondence.

40. You have referred periodically to Deutero-Pauline letters, letters that Paul himself might not have written. What difference does it make if Paul did or did not write these letters?

I discussed this question somewhat in question 2 but did not address its significance there. I suppose from one angle, one could say that it makes little difference. After all, all thirteen letters attributed to Paul are in the Bible. They are all inspired scripture, equally canonical and therefore valuable for Christian teaching. Does it really matter whether Paul is the source of one idea or another, or whether some anonymous author is?

I believe, however, that it does make a difference. For one thing, it is important to reconstruct early Christian history as accurately as possible. Contemporary Christians rely forcefully on what they perceive the Bible does or does not teach, especially with regard to doctrine and morality. It is incumbent upon us, then, to be as accurate as we can in summarizing the biblical teachings and understanding their development over time.

Second, I think we owe it to Paul's legacy to be as fair as we can about what he personally did or did not hold. Christians in every era have blamed him for one perspective or another. Some have charged him with distorting Jesus' teaching, and others have accused him of hating women. Yet if someone was writing in his name under entirely different circumstances, this can help us to distinguish what is or is not genuinely Paul. History has shown us repeatedly that once ideas get into place, they are difficult to dislodge. Our modern perspective and yearning for objectivity, insofar as it can be achieved, demands that we put all our resources to work at discerning the truth as much as possible. In Part Six,

Paul's Ethics, I will try to demonstrate how this works out concretely in several alleged teachings of Paul.

Finally, being able to discern earlier from later NT documents can help provide a proper interpretation of passages. It can also assist with tracing the growth of an idea, such as the development of the concept of "church." It is axiomatic to assert that context is of utmost importance in biblical interpretation. This includes historical, literary, and theological contexts. Each letter must be studied on its own merits and placed in its own diverse contexts. Trying to ascertain who Paul's opponents or conversation partners are in various letters, for instance, can help determine what he meant in some ambiguous or obscure passages. Likewise, this applies if a letter can be shown to be of later origin and from an entirely different historical circumstance.

In sum, although scholars may not be able to reach unanimity or absolute certainty on these questions, I maintain that they are important.

41. You never mentioned the Letter to the Hebrews. Didn't Paul write this letter, too? And who were the "Hebrews"?

The Letter to the Hebrews presents another problem. You will note in your Bible that the title for the Letter to the Hebrews does not mention Paul's name. Already in the early church there was disagreement about whether Paul had written this letter or not. Partly what promoted the idea of Pauline authorship was that some early manuscripts and copies of the NT letters placed Hebrews after Romans or immediately after the other Pauline epistles. In essence, this was authorship by association. Further support came from an incidental mention of the name "Timothy" (Heb 13:23), which was automatically identified with Paul's well-known companion (Rom 16:21; 1 Cor 4:17). The fact that Paul was the best-known letter writer among Christians contributed to the idea as well. In any case, Christians in the East, especially in Alexandria, Egypt, tended to accept Paul as the author of the letter. Christians in the West did not generally accept the idea until the fourth century.

Other factors besides canonical considerations affect the decision to reject Pauline authorship of Hebrews. I suggest you read the letter for yourself after reading one or two of Paul's undisputed letters. I think you will immediately notice a difference. Only the conclusion (Heb 13:18–25) sounds anything like one of Paul's letters. The opening statement is like a formal address on a theological topic. Much of the vocabulary is different from Paul's letters, and there is little connection even with the Deutero-Pauline letters. Its very form looks more like a treatise or a sermon rather than a letter. It lacks the spontaneity and personality of Paul's letters. Finally, the content of Hebrews is quite unique. Nowhere in Paul's letters (or the rest of the NT, for that matter) does one find the notion of the "high priesthood" of Jesus Christ. In short, scholars judge Hebrews to be in a different category altogether. Who the author was is unknown. The oft-quoted judgment of the famous patristic writer Origen sums it up best: "But who wrote the epistle, in truth, God knows!"

This leaves one last element of your question. Who were the Hebrews? The designation of this letter "to the Hebrews" dates only from the second century A.D. It is an unusual designation. One might expect to see the word "Jews" or "Jewish Christians" as the designated recipients. Clearly Hebrews uses the OT with great frequency. It establishes a theological view in which Jesus Christ is compared with many aspects of Judaism and found to be better in every respect. Obviously the readers are presumed to be familiar with the OT, but one cannot know for sure that they were Jewish Christians. Unlike many of Paul's letters, the text also lacks clues that point to a geographical location for its origin. The identity of these "Hebrews," then, remains as anonymous as the author.

42. Is there a difference between a letter and an epistle?

In earlier times it was more common to refer to Paul's correspondence as "epistles" rather than "letters." Somehow the designation seemed more formal. Common parlance often understands epistle as a "long letter." In contemporary church jargon the two words are used interchangeably. A dictionary definition of epistle is simply a "letter, especially a formal one" (*The American Heritage Dictionary* [Boston: Houghton Mifflin, 1991]). This definition hints at the earlier scholarly distinction between a letter and an epistle. People thought of epistles as more formal than letters. Whereas letters were commonplace, written to friends, business partners, and acquaintances, epistles were considered to be written for a broader audience.

It is true that some of the letters in the Pauline tradition have a more formal tone. Letters like Ephesians or Colossians may have been written for broader audiences. Generally, however, Paul's letters are *occasional* letters. That is, they are written to specific groups in specific places on specific occasions. In this sense we can still make a valid distinction between a letter and an epistle. Letters are written on specific occasions; epistles are created for general circumstances. But in contemporary modern English, the distinction has largely been lost. Thus it is appropriate to call Paul's writings letters, but it is not inappropriate to refer to them as epistles. Neither is designating Paul's writings "letters" a devaluation of their worth nor a judgment about their religious value. The lectionary, for instance, introduces readings from NT letters as, "A reading from the Letter of Paul to...." Calling Paul's writings "letters" is simply an acknowledgment of their proper form.

There is one more aspect of the notion of "epistle" that I should mention. You may see or hear the term "catholic epistles" applied to seven NT writings; namely, James; 1 and 2 Peter; 1, 2, and 3 John; and Jude. The designation "catholic epistles" is actually an ancient one, dating to the early patristic period (at least to the third century A.D.). In this case, designating them epistles probably is making a statement that they are indeed broader in scope (more universal) and more formal in tone than most of Paul's letters, whether undisputed or Deutero-Pauline. Some scholars use the term "catholic epistles" with regard to these NT letters because of tendencies toward institutionalization of the church in these later NT documents. They also consider 1 and 2 Timothy and Titus in a similar vein. Some have seen such trends toward increasing bureaucracy in the church as evidence of "catholic" influence. They interpret references to church offices such as deacons, presbyters, and bishops as examples of the church in the later NT period growing into an organization. This designation need not have a pejorative connotation, as it may simply indicate that the church experienced increasing institutionalization as time went on.

43. Does what you are saying mean that Paul's letters really are like letters you write to friends?

Yes, I am saying that Paul's letters are genuinely in the form of personal letters. I might suggest that this is one of the few instances where we are permitted to read someone else's mail! Paul even expects that his letters will be more widely shared (see 1 Thess 5:27; Col 4:16). But I also need to clarify distinctions among Paul's letters.

You will recall in question 38 that the Greco-Roman world knew of many different kinds of letters. Not every letter was personal or friendly. Letters served different purposes. The forms of letters could consequently be different, with each form geared to address given situations that suited the occasion. Paul's letters are such "occasional" letters. Paul wrote them most frequently to respond to specific questions or controversies that had erupted after he had moved on to other geographical regions. I believe a key to understanding each of Paul's letters is to try to understand the individual situation that Paul was trying to address. Unfortunately, modern readers are left to try to reconstruct situations that are now obscured by centuries of history.

Let's take First Corinthians as an example. Paul tells us that at least three factors occasioned his writing this letter to the Corinthians. One was a report given to him by "Chloe's people" about certain situations in Corinth (1 Cor 1:11). Nothing else is known of Chloe outside of this reference. She was either a leader in the Corinthian community or perhaps a resident of Ephesus (from where Paul wrote this letter) who had frequent contacts with people in Corinth, perhaps for reasons of business. The letter does not specifically identify "her people" (literally, "those of Chloe"). Are they members of her family? Slaves or trusted household servants? It is hard to say. At any rate, she sent word to Paul that quarrels had developed among the Corinthians. Paul addresses this issue forthrightly in his letter. This factor becomes essential to keep in the background as one reads about Paul's advice to this divided community.

Another factor was that the Corinthians themselves had sent a letter to Paul (1 Cor 7:1) outlining several issues that had raised questions pertaining to the Christian life. Thus much of Paul's letter focuses on these problems, and we can infer what the situations in Corinth were like from the way Paul formulated his responses. Finally, Paul had discussions with those who had brought the letter to him from Corinth (1 Cor 16:17). He commends them for refreshing his spirit, and they were doubtless able to fill in the details about what was happening in the Corinthian church.

Now you see that all of these factors become important for interpreting this letter. They help clarify that Paul was not simply addressing general issues but specific problems or questions that applied concretely to the situation in Corinth. Unfortunately, we do not have the Corinthian side of the arguments available. The letter they sent has been lost in history. There is no record of Paul's conversations either with Chloe's people or with the Corinthians who brought further information to Paul (Stephanus, Fortunatus, and Achiacus mentioned in 1 Cor 16:17). Thus the

challenge is to reconstruct as much possible—with due caution—
the other side of the conversation in order to understand better
Paul's own statements. This is the nature of occasional letters.

Another example of the personal side of Paul's letters is the
little Letter to Philemon. So small that it has no chapter divisions,
this letter is addressed to an individual named Philemon and other
members of his household and house church (Phlm 1–2). The
issue is over a runaway slave named Onesimus. Paul encountered
him in prison and converted him to Christianity (Phlm 10). Paul
writes this most personal of all his letters to exhort Philemon not
to punish Onesimus in the normal fashion of a runaway slave.
Rather, he was to welcome him back as a Christian "…brother,
beloved especially to me, but even more so to you, as a man and
in the Lord" (Phlm 16 NAB). Reading this letter really is like
eavesdropping on a private conversation. Nonetheless, it is preserved in the NT for all time and has had its own impact in certain
areas of Christian thought.

44. Who preserved Paul's letters and how did they get into the Bible?

If you are asking for names of individuals who preserved
Paul's letters, there is no written record of this. Your question
really gets at the issue of how the canon of sacred scripture came
into being. Christians believe the Holy Spirit guided the entire
process, complex though it was. Paul's letters are certainly an
important part of the formation of the Christian canon. Indeed, his
letters were the earliest NT documents to be collected in order to
be preserved for later generations. Paul occasionally asked that
his letters be read to a wide group of people (1 Thess 5:27), but he
did not envision that we would be reading them two thousand
years later.

Since Paul had many companions and coworkers in the
course of his ministry, any of them could have participated in the
initiative to preserve his letters. Just as the OT prophets before

him, Paul had trusted colleagues and disciples who, especially after his death, desired to have his legacy live on within the Christian community. Today many people do not save their personal correspondence, something that modern historians bemoan. Where would our understanding of much of history be without the testimony of ancient and modern letters that record events, feelings, and personalities of various epochs?

Although the early Christian churches would have understood the "occasional" quality of Paul's letters, there was also much in them that applied in general ways to all Christians. They no doubt recognized special letters, like Romans, as having theological significance far beyond the local community. Paul himself became a forceful figure, at least in his own communities. That alone could have initiated interest in preserving his letters in a collection to be passed on from generation to generation. Eventually some early Christians collected his letters into one group. There is also a functional rationale for ordering the letters as we now have them in the Bible. Because Christians collected their writings in the form of books rather than the Jewish form of scrolls, it was easier to group writings according to size. Thus Paul's letters flow from the longest letter (Romans) to the shortest (Philemon), with Ephesians a bit out of order. They also appear to have been grouped along the division of letters to churches followed by letters to individuals.

A sense of how the canonical process worked is found in First Corinthians. Paul says in two passages, "For I received from the Lord what I also handed on to you..." (1 Cor 11:23; cf. 15:3). This line refers to the oral traditions about the Last Supper and the resurrection of Jesus. These oral traditions, preserved in the preaching of Paul and other apostles in the course of their missionary work (Rom 10:14–15), eventually were collected into writings, the oldest of which are Paul's letters. Christians began to preserve these written communications as the apostles died out and it became clear that Jesus' promised return in the fullness of God's kingdom would be delayed for an indefinite period.

In summary, preserving Paul's letters was a long, complicated process. It began early in the Christian era but it took centuries to be finalized. At least it can be said that by the time of St. Athanasius (A.D. 367), Paul's letters were firmly in place along with the rest of the twenty-seven books of the NT, for Athanasius lists them in an Easter letter declaring the scriptural books accepted as inspired by the Holy Spirit. Keep in mind that no originals of Paul's letters exist. All that remain are copies of copies. Of the some five thousand Greek NT manuscripts in existence, the oldest copy of Paul's letters is found in the Chester Beatty Papyrus (ca. A.D. 200), but there are missing pages in it.

45. Do all of Paul's letters have the same form?

Yes, in general they do. Just as most letters today have a set form to them, letters in the Greco-Roman world were stylized. The basic form included the following sections:

Address and greeting
Thanksgiving
Body (message)
Closing

This outline closely resembles the basic pattern of modern letters with the exception of a specific section on thanksgiving. It was customary in Paul's day to include a special section after the greeting that expressed thanks to the gods and a wish for good health. Paul basically adopts this Greco-Roman style of letter writing but adapts it to his Christian context. His thanksgiving section expresses thanks to God alone or sometimes to God through Jesus Christ (Rom 1:8; 1 Cor 1:4; 1 Thess 1:2). Paul also expands the typical letter format with the resulting structure:

Address and greeting
Thanksgiving
Body (message)
Ethical instruction (paraenesis)
Closing (including travel plans)

It is possible to subdivide this fivefold structure with a variety of other categories. But the basic format holds. A separate section is often discernible in Paul's letters in which he gives specific instructions on Christian moral behavior. This is technically called *paraenesis*. It is ethical exhortation urging his audience to adhere to certain primary Christian principles that apply to various moral situations he addresses. Such ethical instruction can also be scattered throughout the letters, but it is often grouped into one separate section. One should note that this material is not haphazard or an addendum but an integral part of Paul's letters.

An added feature to Paul's letters can be found in different sections but often in the closing. Paul frequently speaks of his travel plans, whether in his desire to come and visit or his intention to carry on his mission farther afield. In Romans, for example, Paul speaks of his intention to go to Spain after his visit to the Roman community (Rom 15:24). In First Corinthians he notifies his congregation that he might stay with them again for awhile (1 Cor 16:6). This feature is another aspect of Paul's letters that makes them so personal.

Paul uses this basic fivefold structure in all his letters with one exception. The Letter to the Galatians does not have a thanksgiving section. Immediately after the greeting (Gal 1:1–5), Paul launches into the body of his letter with harsh words about those in Galatia who are deserting the gospel message. He charges that they have been given bad advice by certain people who are urging the practice of circumcision. Since it is most unusual for Paul not to have a thanksgiving section in his letters, this exclusion signals how upset he is with the Galatians for reverting to elements of their former faith. Even the little letter to Philemon utilizes the basic fivefold structure. A letter like Ephesians, which has more the character of a formal letter to the whole Christian church rather than to one community, can also be structured in this fashion.

46. Which is Paul's most important letter?

Without a doubt, many would say Romans. But in the same breath I should speak to some complications that grow out of your question. I think every professional student of Paul's letters would say that Romans is the most important *theological* letter that Paul wrote. Christians through the ages have recognized the content of this letter as one of the greatest summaries of Christian teaching ever assembled. Romans demonstrates Paul's critical thinking skills, his expertise at expressing clearly his faith, his vision of the impact of Jesus Christ on the world, and his ability to persuade his audience with great conviction. It is also Paul's most systematic letter. In it Paul attempts to synthesize for a community that he did not found and that knew him only by reputation much of what he thought important in the Christian faith.

Yet I am speaking from a rather restricted theological standpoint. To acclaim Romans as the most important Pauline letter is not to denigrate the other letters. In fact, all of Paul letters are important and theological. Both letters to Corinth, for instance, are important for giving hints about what ordinary Christian life was like in Paul's day. The Corinthian correspondence more than any other gives us a glimpse of early Christian traditions such as the celebration of the Eucharist (1 Cor 11), the functions of charisms (1 Cor 12), the importance of the resurrection (1 Cor 15), or a theology of reconciliation (2 Cor 5). Likewise the Thessalonian correspondence describes vividly the problem of the early Christians's expectation of Jesus' second coming (1 Thess 4—5; 2 Thess 2), while Philippians contains one of the most beautiful and profound christological hymns in the early church (chap. 2; but see also the hymn in John 1:1–18). Galatians, too, especially in conjunction with Romans, contains an important exposition on the implications of Christian freedom (chap. 5). My point is that all of Paul's letters are important. Taken together they provide the single greatest testimony of the influence of this one apostolic figure who shaped the course of Christian history.

47. You have spoken of ideas that come from Paul himself. Does he ever quote Jesus in his letters?

Paul is careful to make a distinction between his own teachings and those that come from the Lord. In a passage concerning virgins he says he has "no command of the Lord, but I give my opinion as one who by the Lord's mercy is trustworthy" (1 Cor 7:25). But there are passages that reflect knowledge of Jesus' teachings. Although it is questionable that Paul ever quotes Jesus directly, he nonetheless makes reference to traditions that have come down to him "from the Lord." The most prominent example occurs in 1 Corinthians about the Last Supper. It is clearly from a liturgical setting:

> For I received from the Lord what I also handed on to you, that the Lord Jesus on the night when he was betrayed took a loaf of bread, and when he had given thanks, he broke it and said, "This is my body that is for you. Do this in remembrance of me." In the same way he took the cup also, after supper, saying, "This cup is the new covenant in my blood. Do this, as often as you drink it, in remembrance of me." (1 Cor 11:23–25)

You will recognize immediately how close these words are to the Last Supper accounts in the Synoptic Gospels (Matt 26:26–28; Mark 14:22–24; Luke 22:19–20). Paul's account of the Lord's Supper is in fact the oldest in the NT. Note that he even uses the expression "Lord's supper" (1 Cor 11:20). Paul insists that this tradition must be respected by the Corinthians in the context of their eucharistic gatherings precisely because it is a tradition associated with the Lord Jesus.

Perhaps we should also consider Paul's assertion of the ability to cry out in the Spirit to God "Abba! Father!" (Rom 8:15; Gal 4:6) as evidence that he knew some important traditions about Jesus. Scholars believe that this type of informal address to God is the special way Jesus addressed God in an intimate fashion (Mark 14:36). One could also add that there are likely some echoes of the Sermon on the Mount in Paul's letters (e.g., Rom 12:14; 14:13–14) or other teachings (1 Cor 4:2).

An interesting passage is found in 1 Corinthians 9:14 where Paul says of Christian missionaries, "In the same way, the Lord commanded that the one who proclaims the gospel should live by the gospel" (my translation). It is not known exactly where this command comes from, but it may reflect Jesus' instruction to his disciples that "the laborers deserve their food" (Matt 10:10). He also claims to have commands from the Lord concerning prophetic utterances (1 Cor 14:37), the return of the Lord (1 Thess 4:15), and the prohibition of divorce (1 Cor 7:10). With regard to the latter he goes on to give his own opinion—not from the Lord—that in the case of marriage between a Christian and an unbeliever it may be best in some circumstances to separate (1 Cor 7:12, 15). In other words, Paul seems to take great pains to make a distinction between traditions and teachings he has received, those that originate with the Lord Jesus, and those that express his own opinion.

On the whole, however, there are few passages where Paul quotes Jesus. Of course, there were also no written Gospels to use as resources. There are a number of other passages where Paul makes allusions to Jesus' teachings (e.g., 1 Thess 5:2; 1 Cor 10:27; Rom 14:13). What is surprising is how infrequently Paul speaks about Jesus or his teachings. Not once does Paul recount a parable, something we take for granted as a special teaching technique of Jesus. Nor does he refer to miracles stories that are found to one degree or another in all of the Gospels.

There is even surprising little teaching material from Jesus when one considers the great tracts of teaching found, for instance, in Matthew and Luke. One validly presumes that many of these traditions came to the evangelists by way of oral tradition. They could easily antedate Paul's letters. Why then does Paul make little reference to them? Why is there no teaching of the "Our Father" or the beatitudes? We honestly do not know why Paul left out so many familiar elements of what can be called "the

Jesus tradition." He may well have instructed his congregations in this material and felt no need to repeat it. Most critical for Paul, what was absolutely essential, was not the recollection of Jesus' teachings or deeds, but the significance of his work as risen Lord in the assembly of faithful Christians. We should have "the mind of Christ" (1 Cor 2:16; cf. Rom 11:34 and 8:27) rather than every detail about him.

48. Are you saying that Paul isn't interested in Jesus or that he didn't know much about him?

Not exactly. Keep in mind that an important distinction exists between the "historical Jesus" and the "Christ of faith." The former term refers to the earthly life and ministry of Jesus of Nazareth. The latter term refers to his risen state, the Christian affirmation that he is Lord and Christ. We can explore the first concept by trying to read the NT from an historical vantage point, but the NT is also filled with aspects of the second concept that make it difficult to make absolutely certain pronouncements about the historical Jesus.

It is a big step to move from saying that Paul does not often refer to Jesus in his earthly state to saying that he was not interested in him or did not know much about him. It is difficult to imagine that one who had direct contact with people like Cephas, James the brother of the Lord, and John would not have had considerable knowledge of Jesus of Nazareth. In fact, Paul summarizes in certain passages what he knows about Jesus. He affirms that Jesus was a Jew "descended from [King] David according to the flesh" (Rom 1:3). Paul also acknowledges that Jesus was "born of a woman" (Gal 4:4). At some length he focuses on the passion, death, and resurrection of Jesus done in accordance with the OT scriptures (1 Cor 15:3–8), noting that he was betrayed (1 Cor 11:23) but never naming the betrayer. He says Jesus was crucified (1 Cor 1:23; Gal 3:1), died (1 Cor 15:3), and was buried (1 Cor 15:4), but then miraculously was raised from the dead (1 Cor 15:4).

Paul is interested in Jesus, for he urges the Corinthians not to follow after someone who "comes and proclaims another Jesus than the one we proclaimed" (2 Cor 11:4). Yet notice how seldom Paul speaks of the name Jesus without any other designation such as *Lord Jesus, Christ* Jesus, the *Lord* Jesus Christ, and so on. He is interested in Jesus, not in the stories of Jesus as a human being. Rather he emphasizes the larger story of Jesus that encompasses both his earthly life and ministry and his ongoing heavenly intervention.

None of the Pauline letters mentions Jesus of *Nazareth*. When the name Jesus is used it most often *implies* one aspect or another of the risen Jesus as Christ and Lord (1 Cor 12:3; 2 Cor 4, 10, 11; Phil 2:10; 1 Thess 1:10; 4:14). Only in Galatians does Paul use the name of Jesus in a direct reference to Jesus' earthly life. There he says, "...for I carry the marks *(stigmata)* of Jesus branded on my body" (Gal 6:17). While this expression clearly refers to the marks of Jesus' crucifixion, Paul implies even here an understanding of Jesus as the vindicated crucified Lord, for other manuscript traditions add the titles Lord and Christ. This information offers a clue to Paul's real concern. The Pauline letters speak frequently of all the significant christological aspects of Jesus Christ as vindicated by God in the resurrection. Paul does not discount the life and ministry of Jesus. Rather, the most important facet of his understanding of Jesus is that he is the risen Lord who appeared to him, commissioned him, and who now continually calls people to faith through baptism. Paul's "gospel" centers, then, not on retelling the stories of Jesus of Nazareth but on proclaiming the message of the Lord Jesus Christ and his significance.

49. Are you implying that Paul's understanding of the word "gospel" does not refer to a book about Jesus? If not, what does Paul mean by it?

Yes, I am saying that Paul does not use the word "gospel" to refer to the NT Gospels. The Pauline letters employ the word "gospel" (Greek *euaggelion,* from which our word "evangelist" derives) fifty-six times in a variety of contexts. If one adds the verbal form, "to announce good news" or "to proclaim," there are an additional twenty-one occurrences. Clearly the word is popular in Paul's letters, especially in the seven undisputed letters. In fact, Paul was the first Christian writer ever to employ the term in his writings, but his use of the term implies that other Christians were already familiar with it. Paul's letters use the term more frequently than any other NT writer. To get at its meaning we need to review the variety of expressions Paul uses.

In the secular language of Paul's day, the word "gospel" simply meant "good news" or "news of victory." The expression often appeared in the context of an announcement of some political importance, such as victory in battle or the birth of a royal heir. In the Septuagint (the Greek translation of the Hebrew scriptures used by Paul and others), it also refers to the announcement of God's victory over evil. In Paul's writings the most frequent use of the word is the absolute form, "the gospel." It also occurs with modifiers, such as "the gospel of God" or "the gospel of Christ." All three expressions are alternated in one letter, First Thessalonians, indicating that there is an interrelationship between the expressions (1 Thess 1:5; 2:2, 4, 8, 9; 3:2). There is also a nuance of meaning. The "gospel of God" refers to the fact that God is the *origin* of the good news of salvation in Jesus Christ, whereas "the gospel of Christ" means the good news *about* Jesus Christ. In general, the absolute use of the word is a shorthand version of referring to the "Christ-event," that is, God's gracious action toward humanity in sending his Son Jesus Christ to be the world's salvation from sin and death. Jesus' birth, life, public ministry, passion, death, resurrection, and return to the Father are all summed up in the word "gospel." The term, then, is primarily a christological term. It focuses on the person of Jesus Christ. In at least two passages, Paul gives a thumbnail sketch of the essentials of his "gospel" that shows the full effects of the Christ-event (see Rom 5:1–11; 2 Cor 5:11–21).

What are some of the significant statements Paul makes about his understanding of the gospel? He insists that it comes from God and concerns God's Son (Rom 1:1, 3, 9; Gal 1:11). Paul is not ashamed to proclaim the gospel because it contains a message of salvation for all humankind (Rom 1:16). Sometimes he seems almost possessive and highly protective of the gospel. He calls it "my gospel" (Rom 16:25; cf. "our gospel," 1 Thess 1:5), and his duty to proclaim it even supersedes the duty to baptize (1 Cor 1:17). So strongly does he feel impelled to proclaim the gospel message of salvation that nothing can prevent him from doing it (1 Cor 9:16). Even his sufferings do not hinder the gospel; on the contrary, they help to spread it (Phil 1:12; 1 Thess 2:2).

There can be no alternative gospel. (Note that in Paul's letters the word is only used in the singular.) There is only one gospel and it is about Jesus Christ (2 Cor 11:4; Gal 1:7–9). In one instance, Paul uses gospel in its simplest sense as the proclamation of good news. He mentions that "I had been entrusted with the gospel for the uncircumcised, just as Peter had been entrusted with the gospel for the circumcised" (Gal 2:7). This is not a division of the gospel itself but the separate task of proclaiming the one gospel to two different sets of people, Jews and Gentiles. Throughout his letters Paul is concerned with protecting "the truth of the gospel" (Gal 2:5, 14). He abhors any attempt to compromise what is essential in the faith. He also states that the gospel must be proclaimed boldly (Phil 1:14) but that it is more than simply stating a message in words. He reminds the Thessalonians, for instance, that "our message of the gospel came to you not in word only, but also in power and in the Holy Spirit and with full conviction; just as you know what kind of persons we proved to be among you for your sake" (1 Thess 1:5).

Paul's understanding of the gospel of Jesus Christ is simultaneously single-minded and yet multifaceted. For Paul, the focus on the gospel is the direct result of his call by God to be a missionary who evangelizes the world with conviction and power.

50. How does Paul treat the OT in his writings?

Paul and all the early Christians knew the OT as the only sacred scriptures in their tradition. Of course, it was not known as the OT. These sacred books were simply called "scripture" or "the writings" (2 Tim 3:16). The OT in Paul's day existed in two editions. One edition was in Hebrew, the other in Greek. The Hebrew version existed long before the Greek version and was the mainstay of Judaism. After the influence of the Hellenistic world became so prominent, and once Jews went into far-flung parts of the empire (the "diaspora"), a need arose to translate the Hebrew scriptures into Greek. Greek was the main language of the Greco-Roman world even though Latin was used in Rome for government business. Already in the second century B.C. the Jews made a Greek translation of their Hebrew scriptures so that the Jews in the diaspora would be able to utilize them in daily life. This translation is known as the Septuagint (abbreviated LXX, the Roman numeral 70) after the legend that seventy different translators all produced the same translation after working on it for seventy days.

Paul probably knew both editions of the scriptures. His primary language, however, was Greek, and he shows a preference for quoting or alluding to the Septuagint. Altogether Paul quotes the OT more than one hundred times, with many more allusions to different passages. The Letter to the Romans summarizes Paul's perspective on the sacred writings of Israel: The prophetic writings have been fulfilled in Jesus Christ and God's mysterious plan of salvation has been revealed in him (Rom 1:2; 16:25–26). This was Paul's view of the fulfillment of Israel's scriptures, but he recognized the sad fact that his Jewish sisters and brothers often did not accept this message (Rom 9—11). When he quotes scripture Paul sometimes introduces it with a question or a phrase like, "What does the scripture say?" or "As scripture says..." (Rom 4:3; 9:17; 10:11; Gal 4:30). More often, though, Paul simply quotes or alludes to scripture in the midst of his own writing. So important is this perspective that Paul occasionally added a line, "according to the scriptures," to earlier tradition that he quotes (1 Cor 15:3–4).

Paul's use of the OT embraces more than one method. By and large, he employs a style of interpretation that scholars call "rabbinic midrash." In other words, Paul applied typical interpretive tools that were common to the rabbis of his day.

51. Can you describe in more detail what you mean by this "rabbinic" style of interpretation?

There is no one rabbinic style of interpretation. Rather, the rabbis—those trained in the tools of interpreting the sacred writings of the Jews—employed a variety of approaches to make the writings contemporary. Rabbis poured over the scriptures in earnest in order to try to discern God's message for their own day. Paul likewise knew the scriptures very well. It would not have been unusual for rabbis and those with Paul's education to memorize great tracts of scripture. At times, Paul may be vague about what specific passage he has in mind. This method of using scripture can sound very foreign to our ears. The rabbinic method regularly took a passage out of its original context, read it literally or figuratively, and adapted it to another time and context. This approach often gave the quotation an entirely different twist than found in the original.

This is a more free-floating type of biblical interpretation. An example can be found in 1 Corinthians 10:1–4. Paul recalls Moses leading the Israelites through the wilderness and brings up the image of water from the rock (see Exod 17:1–7). He translates this into a baptismal image and then pronounces that "the rock was Christ." Here Paul uses both a familiar OT story and probably Jewish legends that grew up about it. In fact, this reality poses problems for present readers of Paul's letters. At times it is impossible to know what other sources Paul is using to supplement the biblical images he uses.

Another method Paul employs is to invoke certain OT figures when he quotes scripture. This is a "typological" use of the

OT. He uses Israel's ancient ancestors like Adam, Moses, Abraham, Sarah, Elijah, and so on as models to illustrate some aspect of the Christian faith. These figures then become for Paul a *type* or an image that conveys a message to his audience and ultimately to contemporary Christians. Thus Christ is a new Adam (1 Cor 15:45), and Abraham the premier model of faith (Rom 4:16). In typically rabbinic fashion, then, Paul used the OT with great regularity. He did it from a Christian perspective. He viewed Israel's sacred writings as the repository of God's will. This was not solely for Israel but also for the prophetic fulfillment of Israel's hopes in the person and message of Jesus Christ. It was a living, breathing word that gave life to his people. Paul firmly believed in adapting the OT to suit his theological message for his congregations. He thought the fulfillment of the OT vision had already come upon the world but that he and his communities were living in the final days of that fulfillment. We sometimes have to read very carefully to understand clearly what Paul meant by quoting or alluding to certain OT passages, but we can be sure that Paul thought he was interpreting the scriptures correctly for his day.

52. Paul frequently seems to be arguing with people. Who were Paul's opponents?

That depends on which letter you are referring to. You are right to observe that Paul often seems to be in the throes of an argument with somebody. But his discussion partners (a more friendly, but less telling, way of viewing them; they are adversaries) are different in each instance. Unfortunately we have only one half of the conversation before us. The actual arguments or responses of Paul's discussion partners are lost to history. With only one side of the discussion available, you can imagine how difficult it can be to reconstruct who the other parties were and what their side of the discussion may have looked like. With this understood, let's look at what scholars say about some of Paul's conversation partners.

Not every letter of Paul shows evidence of strong disagreements between Paul and somebody. Some letters have a more negative tone than others. Romans, Philemon, and First Thessalonians are relatively peaceful letters. There are issues in them that Paul tackles head on, but they do not have the sharp tones of First and Second Corinthians, Galatians, and even Philippians.

At first glance First Thessalonians seems to be a peaceful letter. The tone of this letter is both thankful and hopeful. Paul, mirroring good pastoral practice, highly commends their faith because they had become "a model for all the believers in Macedonia and Achaia" (1 Thess 1:7 NAB). But one can detect evidence of a problem in the Thessalonian community that Paul tries to address. Paul says that they are suffering "from your own compatriots" just as the church in Judea suffered from Jewish opposition (1 Thess 2:14). Whoever these people were, they planted seeds of doubt among the Thessalonians that Paul was no better than a common huckster of cheap philosophy, out to make a living off of them. Paul reminds them that he worked for his own living while he was in their midst (1 Thess 2:9), and he urges them to "work with your hands" in order not to burden anyone (1 Thess 4:11–12). An additional problem was that some members of the community had died. This seriously shook their hope in the resurrection. So Paul reminds them with his typical apocalyptic view that the day of the Lord will come suddenly "like a thief in the night" (1 Thess 5:1–8). They are to remain hopeful and vigilant.

The Corinthian correspondence contains quite a different perspective about the kind of problems Paul had to deal with. The primary issue in First Corinthians was the existence of factions within the Corinthian community (1 Cor 1:10–14). There was also a host of other specific issues about which the Corinthians themselves wanted Paul's opinion. Questions included: mistaking human wisdom for God's wisdom (1 Cor 2), sexual immorality (1 Cor 5—6), some members scandalizing others in the community by eating meat previously involved in pagan worship (1 Cor 8 and 10), disrespect for the eucharistic celebrations (1 Cor 11), and exaggerating charismatic gifts (1 Cor 12—13). These were internal matters that Paul seeks to remedy. Second Corinthians reveals a different situation. Outsiders have arrived in Corinth who started preaching a message different from Paul's and boasting of their superiority. Paul ironically refers to these people as "super-apostles" (2 Cor 11:5; 12:11). Paul strongly defends his ministry while emphasizing that true wisdom comes from God. This letter also demonstrates that Paul had undergone serious emotionally charged exchanges with the Corinthians through a series of letters, visits, and word-of-mouth interchanges. Finally, Paul and the Corinthians reconciled (2 Cor 5).

The Letter to the Galatians wins the prize for the most vehement of Paul's letters. As I mentioned earlier, it is the only letter that excludes a thanksgiving section. Paul did not feel positively about the outside opposition that had arrived in Galatia after he had left. The exact identity of these opponents is hidden, but the letter makes clear that they favored circumcision. They appear to be Jewish Christians holding on to some Jewish practices that Paul has recognized as no longer valid for followers of Jesus Christ. They have often been called (inaccurately) "Judaizers," but a better term might simply be "circumcisers" or the "circumcision party." Paul considers them agitators who pervert the gospel (Gal 1:7). Paul roundly condemns their "different gospel" that disturbs the Galatians (Gal 1:6–7) and their literal adherence to the law (Gal 5:1–4). His argument climaxes in a vehement and sarcastic wish; namely, that they would castrate themselves in the process of circumcision (Gal 5:12). Paul could certainly be direct!

Even Philippians, a letter whose chief tone is joy, contains evidence of some opposition. Outsiders have troubled the community with religious ideas that oppose Paul's teaching (Phil 3:2). They were likely Jewish Christians influenced by Hellenistic philosophy. Paul refers the Philippians back to the model of Christ, the need for humility and for setting their hearts on the life that is to come in God's kingdom rather than in this earthly life.

In each instance Paul's conversation partners and the situations he addressed are distinctive. We should not join all of Paul's adversaries together into a unified front. Sometimes they were outsiders, sometimes insiders. Some were Jewish, others were Jewish Christians or Gentiles. Some held philosophies or pagan religious ideas totally opposed to the new Christian understanding. Some wanted to hold on to specific Jewish practices, while others simply misunderstood the implications of the gospel message. In any case, Paul tried his best to respond to these difficulties as they arose. When we read Paul's letters, it is wise to take these factors into account.

53. You have mentioned before that Paul's letters show some influence from Greek philosophy. Can you give some examples?

Numerous passages hint that Greek philosophical influence provided a backdrop for what Paul says. Three examples will suffice.

Paul's description of the harsh conditions of apostles (1 Cor 4:9–13) mimics a popular philosophical stance in his day. The major difference, however, is that Paul emphasizes "we are fools for the sake of Christ" (1 Cor 4:10). In another passage Paul urges the Thessalonians to live more and more by the ideal of love,

> ...to aspire to live quietly, to mind your own affairs, and to work with your hands, as we directed you, so that you may behave properly toward outsiders and be dependent on no one. (1 Thess 4:11–12)

These words echo popular Stoic teaching about the need for an independent lifestyle. Again, however, Paul adapts such a notion to meet the immediate circumstances. Some of the Thessalonians were under a misunderstanding that they were already living the resurrected life and no longer needed to work. He corrects their notion with proper guidance to live in a way that builds up the community rather than burdens it. Paul's larger picture is always the Christian context. He is not interested in mere philosophical wisdom. In fact, elsewhere he sharply warns the Corinthian community to avoid worldly wisdom because compared to God's folly, it amounts to nothing (1 Cor 2:6–14).

A third example comes from Greek rhetorical techniques common in Paul's day. I have pointed out earlier (question 5) that Paul used some literary devices common to certain Greek philosophical schools to bolster his argumentation. Primary among these is the "diatribe." In common English parlance a diatribe usually refers to an angry outburst, but that is not what the Greek rhetorical concept was about. Rather, a diatribe involved carefully argued discussions in order to try to defeat an opponent's position and win over followers. Let's look in Romans for an example of this technique.

In Romans 2:1–6 Paul addresses the issue of God's righteous judgment on humanity and the impropriety of people passing judgment on others. This is part of Paul's introduction in Romans that shows that all humanity, both Jew and Gentile—despite their respective advantages and disadvantages—is sinful and in need of God's salvation. Paul's argument then proceeds in four stages at the beginning of chapter 2:

1. Paul makes an opening statement that passing judgment on others actually condemns oneself (v. 1).
2. Then Paul states the argument of his adversaries: "We know that God's judgment on those who do such things is in accordance with the truth." To introduce this quotation, the NRSV adds the phrase "You say...," because the Greek text has no quotation marks, and one can determine only by context that this is not Paul's thought but that of his adversaries (v. 2).
3. Next Paul refutes their statement with a set of three rhetorical questions that point out the weakness of the adversaries' position. The implication from them is that passing judgment will not mitigate their own eventual

fate of being judged nor alleviate their desire for their sense of human justice despite God's more generous mercy (vv. 3–4).

4. Finally, Paul concludes that God's righteous judgment will come upon all on judgment day, "For he will repay according to each one's deeds..." (vv. 5–6).

One should note that it is not always easy to determine from the Greek text what words or phrases belong to Paul and which ones represent the thought of Paul's adversaries. Context is the most important determining factor. In any case, Paul was adept at utilizing this common Greek rhetorical tool to make his point effectively. (For other examples using different techniques common to the diatribe, e.g., rhetorical questions or imaginary conversation partners, see Rom 2:17–24; 3:1–9; 9:19–21; 11:17–24.)

FIVE

———————————

PAUL'S THEOLOGY

54. Where did Paul's theological ideas come from? Are they original to him?

Paul is one of the most original thinkers in the NT. Yet there were also many influences upon Paul's theological and ethical thought.

Theologically Paul was influenced primarily by Judaism. His presuppositions are right out of first-century Jewish traditions. His belief in monotheism, his understanding that human beings are naturally sinful and require salvation, his emphasis on living righteously, his use of OT figures as models of faith, his rabbinic style of scriptural interpretation—all find a comfortable home in Judaism. He did not limit his use of such ideas simply to repeating what had been previously said. He adapted Jewish traditions to his new perspective as an apostle. He refined them, reinterpreted them, and applied them to the new circumstances of faith in Jesus Christ.

Some have wondered whether Paul received his main theological ideas from his conversion experience. A few have conjectured that Paul got *all* of his theology from that one experience. That may be exaggerated. Paul clearly recognizes that his conversion was a revelatory experience (Gal 2:2). God revealed to him the mysteries that had been previously hidden (Rom 16:25). His experience of the risen Lord (1 Cor 9:1; 15:5–8) gave him a personal understanding of Jesus' suffering for the kingdom. But Paul's thought is too broad and too tied to varied circumstances to think that he received a unified theological vision in one revelatory experience. More likely Paul's personal experience of the risen Lord infused him with boldness and confidence. It gave Paul a personal taste of both the suffering and the glory that he would endure for the sake of proclaiming the gospel. It allowed him to address concretely each issue that would come his way in encounters with his communities, but it did not provide him ready-made answers to all life's issues.

Another important influence on Paul's thought was Greek philosophy. A variety of influential philosophical schools existed in Paul's day. They were quite attractive to some diaspora Jews and to a multitude of Gentiles. Most famous were the Stoics and the Cynics. Stoics promoted the notion that human life was controlled by divine forces that required tranquil surrender to these higher powers in order to be truly free. Paul shows some familiarity with Stoic ideas in his concept of freedom and conscience. However, Paul modifies such ideas. Freedom for the Stoics meant self-sufficiency and detachment from life's harshness; for Paul it is a free gift of God that binds one to Christ in living a life of love.

Cynics were wandering teachers who tried to appeal to the common people. They were homeless itinerants whose self-designation came from the Greek word for "dog" *(kyōn),* a name the populace applied to them in a sarcastic manner. They proudly spoke of living independently by means of "nature," and Paul possibly adopts one of their manners of speaking when he talks of "boldly" proclaiming the gospel (Rom 15:15; 2 Cor 3:12). As we saw earlier, Paul's method of discourse owes something to both the Cynics and Stoics. They used a rhetorical device called the *diatribe,* in which the arguments one wanted to refute were placed on the lips of a hypothetical opponent (see Rom 2:21–24; 3:1–10). Diatribes often contained rhetorical questions with anticipated answers that allowed false understandings to be rejected, a method Paul was fond of using (see question 53).

Another influence on Paul's thought was early Christian tradition. Knowing exactly what these resources were is difficult because Paul's writings themselves are the primary source. But in instances like the famous hymn in Philippians (2:6–11), Paul uses earlier Christian material and adapts it to his own purposes.

Despite these various influences on Paul's thought, we have to admit an incredible originality in his letters. He was consistent with other believers in making the person of Jesus Christ utterly central to his preaching. Nothing in the Jewish or Hellenistic world prepared them for the uniqueness of the cross and resurrection of Jesus Christ. His understanding of concepts like justification by faith, the church as the body of Christ, the universal message of salvation as God's free gift in his Son, are also uniquely Christian ideas. In other words, Paul's theological thought was a combination of what he knew from his background and education, as well as what he had experienced in his newfound faith.

55. Does any one letter summarize Paul's ideas?

The closest that one comes to a general summary is the Letter to the Romans, but even it displays the characteristics of being a situational letter. Most scholars judge Romans to be the most comprehensive and synthetic of all Paul's letters, but it does not develop every idea common to Paul's thought. The breadth of Romans is impressive. In it Paul discusses justification, faith, hope, love, sin and its consequences, grace, freedom and slavery, power, salvation, the body of Christ, the relation of the Jews and Gentiles, reconciliation, and so on. Romans, however, does not speak to Paul's call to "imitation" of himself as do his other letters, probably because he did not establish the community and had no substantial personal acquaintance with them. He avoids using strongly familial expressions with them also for the same reason. He writes to them as a fellow believer rather than as a parent to one's children.

If Romans were Paul's only letter to survive, we would still have a great deal of knowledge about Paul's thought. However, we would also lack such eloquent passages as the oldest accounts of the Last Supper (1 Cor 11) and the resurrection (1 Cor 15), the extended metaphor on the body of Christ (1 Cor 12), the poetic reflection on love (1 Cor 13), the eloquent reflection on reconciliation (2 Cor 5), the personal account of the Council of Jerusalem (Gal 2), the great christological hymn (Phil 2), and others. All of

Paul's letters are important for trying to pull together the diverse threads of Paul's thought in order to get the "big picture."

56. Can you summarize Paul's main teaching?

That is a challenging or even an impossible task. Every interpreter of Paul would address your question in a different manner. By and large, scholars have tended to reduce Paul's main teaching to one idea or another, probably with the notion of justification by faith taking first place. But let's step back a moment to consider what your question is really asking.

Paul's letters were written over a span of more than ten years. They were based on a lengthy ministry of preaching the gospel message in an extraordinary variety of circumstances and to diverse groups of people. In addition, his main themes covered a very broad arena of theological ideas, such as the Christian virtues of faith, hope, and love; Jesus Christ as Lord and Savior of the world; God's free gift of salvation; the challenge of living in true Christian freedom; and so on. Is it really possible to reduce Paul's teaching to one quick summary?

For centuries scholars have tried to digest Paul's thought and summarize it in a consistent fashion. They often seek the "central" thought of Paul. Scholars have settled on such concepts as justification by faith, reconciliation, christological soteriology (i.e., the salvation achieved by Christ), apocalypticism, and the ultimate triumph of God, or simply the person of Jesus Christ himself. The results are often impressive. There are always new and sophisticated presentations of Paul's message appearing and claiming to capture in essence what Paul teaches. As admirable as the task is, I am wary of any claim to summarize Paul's teaching in a formula or a "Cliff's notes" version. I don't think Paul's teaching can be reduced to one main idea, even though I would agree that certain Pauline concepts are more important than others.

57. Does Paul have a particular view of God that influences his theology?

Paul's understanding of God (*theo*logy in its literal meaning) can be divided into two categories: implicit and explicit. *Implicitly,* Paul's view of God is rooted in OT theology. His frequent quotations and allusions from the OT provide sufficient testimony for this. Although he does not always express his understanding overtly, his understanding of God is based on that expressed in the Jewish scriptures. Specifically, I point to three major areas of implicit understanding in Paul's letters.

1. God is creator and sustainer of all creation and is thus all-powerful. Foundational to all of Paul's thought is his belief that God created the universe and continues to sustain it (1 Cor 8:6). The Genesis story of creation is a backdrop to Paul's worldview (Gen 1:1–2:25; 2 Cor 4:6). In contrast to pagan theories, Jewish theology understood creation to be a gracious act of God. Creation is essentially good; only human weakness and sin mar it. God has power over all creation, yet God grants human beings free will. God reigns from heaven, but human beings struggle on earth. Creation nevertheless can reveal the grandeur and power of God (Rom 1:20).

2. God is unique and entirely distinct from pagan gods. Paul is monotheistic, believing that God is one, holy, and wholly "other" (Gal 3:20; 1 Cor 8:4; Eph 4:4–6; cf. Deut 6:4; Ps 99:1–5). In contrast to the Greco-Roman religions of Paul's day, Jewish thought emphasized that there could be only one God (Exod 20:2–6). Israel struggled constantly in its history with the temptation to idolatry, turning away from the one, true God.

God is also indivisible, and being totally "other" means that God is transcendent and incomparable to anything else in human experience. Only God is holy (i.e., set apart, sacred), and human beings cannot compare to God's holiness (Isa 6:3–5). Even God's mysterious name revealed to Moses, Yahweh (Exod 3:14; "I AM WHO I AM"), speaks of the "otherness" of the God of Israel.

3. God is the God of Abraham, Isaac, and Jacob, a God of the covenant (Exod 3:6, 15). God acts in human history, and God chooses to enter into a relationship with a chosen people, i.e., Israel, who are called out of love to be peculiarly God's own (Deut 7:7–9). This covenantal relationship imposed certain obligations on Israel, especially in the form of the "torah" given to Moses (Exod 20:1–21). The chosen people struggled to remain faithful to them (Exod 32), however, and often lapsed, despite God's continual fidelity (Ps 105:7–11). This situation led to the expectation of and need for a messiah who would embody a new type of covenant (Jer 31:31– 34).

All of these notions, among others, are found in the OT and are commonplace in the Jewish theological thought of Paul's day. Paul occasionally speaks of or alludes to these ideas in his writings, but they are always assumed in the background.

Paul also has much to say about God *explicitly.* The frequency with which he mentions God, whether in prayerful or liturgical formulations, in exhortations and ethical teachings, or in theological explanations, shows that his understanding of God permeates his thought. I will point out four major areas of Paul's explicit notion of God.

1. God is a savior and redeemer who has a mysterious plan of salvation for the world (Rom 16:25; Eph 1:3–10; 1 Tim 1:1). Since all people are sinners, all need to be saved; and only God's grace can save (Rom 3:9, 23–25). God's plan encompasses the salvation of both Israel and the Gentiles (Rom 11:25–27). For Paul, of course, Jesus Christ is the fulfillment of this plan, for he is the "Savior"; he is God's agent of salvation, for by his sacrifice on the cross the whole world has been saved (Rom 5:6, 8–9; Gal 1:4; 2:20; 1 Tim 1:15).

2. God is "Father," and believers are consequently "brothers and sisters" to one another. Although some perceive "father" language for God as excessively patriarchal and antiquated, it is part of the revealed Judeo-Christian tradition and cannot be shunned. (For an overview of this complex issue, see R. D. Witherup, *A*

Liturgist's Guide to Inclusive Language [Collegeville, Minn.: Liturgical Press, 1996].) To speak of God in these human terms is to see God as a person. God is not simply a force in the universe or a philosophical idea. God loves and cares for his children. As a community of faithful, believers are part of God's "family," and Paul urges his readers to treat one another with due respect. They are to greet one another "with a holy kiss" (1 Cor 16:20; 2 Cor 13:12; 1 Thess 5:26) that represents their participation in the fellowship of the family of God.

As with any parent, God desires only the best for his offspring (Rom 8:28–30; 2 Cor 1:3), but God must also occasionally reprimand and call them to accountability (Rom 2: 2; 1 Cor 11:32). God also desires that his children be forgiven. God wishes to reconcile the entire world (2 Cor 5:17–21) and God will remain faithful to all his promises (2 Cor 1:18–20). God is a person who reveals himself to human beings in a variety of ways. God is first and foremost the Father of Jesus, who is God's "Son" (Rom 1:3; 1 Cor 1:9; 2 Cor 1:19; Gal 1:1). God is also the Father of all those who believe in and follow Jesus Christ ("our Father"; 1 Cor 1:3; 2 Cor 1:2; Gal 1:3–4; 3:26). The Holy Spirit, in fact, allows us to address God in the personal and intimate Aramaic name "Abba" (Rom 8:15; Gal 4:6; cf. Mark 14:36). There are clearly hints of trinitarian thought in Paul (e.g., 2 Cor 13:13), but we must remember that Paul would not have had the benefit of later philosophical and theological distinctions that expanded our understanding of the Trinity as three distinct persons in one Godhead.

3. God's wisdom and knowledge are beyond full human comprehension, and yet God has revealed this wisdom in Jesus Christ (1 Cor 1:18–25; 2:6–16). For Paul, there is a clear contrast between human wisdom and God's. In a Greco-Roman world enamored of philosophy and the achievements of human thought, Paul taught that humanity needed to remain humble with regard to their intellectual achievements (Rom 1:21–22). Human beings constantly tend to forget that they are creatures, not the Creator

(Rom 1:25). Paul's exercise of his ministry is out of the conviction that he is calling people back to creatureliness.

No one can ultimately plumb the depths of the mystery of God (Rom 11:33–35), yet God has granted us "the mind of Christ" (1 Cor 2:16). Indeed, for Paul, God's wisdom shows itself most clearly in paradox. The cross is folly to the world, but in God's eyes it is salvation (1 Cor 1:22–25). The world despises weakness, yet in God's eyes weakness is true strength (2 Cor 12:10). According to Paul, God's ways do not make sense in human terms, but Jesus Christ has revealed this secret knowledge and incarnated it in his life, death, and resurrection.

4. God is filled with awesome glory and majesty (Rom 15:7; Phil 1:11). This idea, rooted in the OT (Exod 24:16–17; Isa 6:3; Pss 19:1; 29:1–4), shows how mindful Paul is of God's "otherness." Paul's ministry is meant to reflect God's glory. It leads people back to the source of their very existence, to God alone. Sometimes Paul expresses his appreciation of God's glory and majesty in the form of a prayer or doxology (exclamation of praise, from the Greek word for "glory" [*doxa*]; Rom 11:33–36; 16:27; Phil 4:20).

These are not the only ideas of God in Paul's letters, but they are key to Paul's thought. Paul clearly perceived his ministry as divinely ordained. God was the source of that ministry, and its final goal. Paul's evangelization was at the service of God's plan, revealed in Jesus Christ, and unfolding in the apostolic ministry of the church (1 Cor 4:1).

58. Does Paul have a distinctive view of salvation history?

I think Paul has a distinctive view of salvation history that undergirds his message. I offer a summary here. Paul reflects traditional Jewish belief that God has a "mysterious plan" *(mystērion)* for the universe. Humans cannot know all of its secrets, yet God has revealed elements of the plan through Jesus Christ. Paul's vision of God's plan extends sweepingly from creation to the parousia, the second coming of Jesus Christ. In typically Jewish fashion, he uses the scope of OT thought to explain that God created all that exists and that it was originally good. Adam was the progenitor of the human race. He embodied God's desires for the human race but, unfortunately, became the vehicle for sin and death entering the world.

Abraham became the father of faith and the stellar example of faith when God called him into a covenant relationship. The chosen people emerged as God's special people, but the situation of sin endured until Moses, when God decided to provide the law as a means of helping the people live up to their calling. The law did not accomplish the task. God chose instead to act definitively by sending his own Son to be a Savior. In his obedience to his Father's will by accepting death on a cross and being vindicated by the resurrection, Jesus Christ brought salvation to the world and formed a new community founded, not on obedience to the law, but on obedience to faith in Christian freedom. This community of faith, brought together by baptism and nourished by brotherly and sisterly love, is called to evangelize the world and bring others to Christ. In the midst of this ministry, they await in hope and in faith the return of Christ in glory, when the fullness of God's plan will be revealed. Only then will the judgment take place in which the saints, those who have remained faithful, will receive their eternal reward, while those who have not will receive damnation.

From our perspective, so much of Paul's thought has influenced traditional Christian teaching that we might not be aware of how foundational his ideas were historically. His view of salvation is not unique, but his ideas were very early and influenced the development of later Christian teaching. A distinctive element in his plan is the emphasis on eschatological urgency. He believed that God's plan was being revealed very rapidly and that the anticipated events of the last days (the eschaton) would happen quickly and within the lifetime of either himself or his colleagues. Christians eventually lost that eschatological edge, but it remains an element in all Christian teaching, even if it has been conceived as an event in the distant, indeterminate future.

59. What is grace, according to Paul?

Grace (Greek *charis*) is one of those mysterious terms that defies concrete definition. Nonetheless, it features heavily in Paul's letters, occurring some one hundred times in all thirteen letters attributed to Paul. The Letter to the Romans contains the most numerous occurrences of the term (twenty-three times), so there can be little doubt that it is an important theological concept. However, it also functions in various ways.

A common use of the term is in the greeting and conclusion of each letter. The expression is often a prayerful wish, "Grace to you and peace from God our Father…" or "The grace of our Lord Jesus Christ be with you…" (1 Cor 1:3; cf. 2 Cor 1:2; Rom 1:7; 16:20; Phil 4:23). It expresses a desire that God's (and/or Christ's) power, blessing, and beneficence should come upon the readers/hearers of Paul's letters. In fact, its most basic idea is that God is gracious toward human beings. Grace is an attribute of God and therefore also of his Son Jesus Christ. It is a "power" of God that God bestows on people; it has the power to transform one's life (see 2 Cor 12:9 where Paul connects grace to the transformation of weakness into strength). It embodies God's beneficent and steadfast attitude toward human beings. Grace is essentially God's favor toward humanity. It comes from God but also draws us closer to God. It is a participation in God's life here on earth. It might be likened to a "sacred energy" that enables human beings to conform more closely to God's will.

Although for Catholics grace is something that can be quantified and distinguished (e.g., distinctions between actual and sanctifying grace), for Paul grace is more broadly tied to God's gift of salvation to the world. Grace is the enabler of salvation and justification (Rom 3:24; 5:17). It is a free gift from God (Rom 5:15; 12:3; 15:15; 1 Cor 1:4), and as such, it is also tied to the various "gifts" (*charismata,* from the same Greek root) of the Spirit that are bestowed upon the members of the church (Rom 12:6). Grace is, in some measure, opposed to the works of the law (Rom 6:15; 11:6) and to sin (Rom 5:20–21), but it is also something that one can fall away from (Gal 1:6; 5:4). For Paul himself, he asserts that his very call as an apostle was through God's grace (1 Cor 15:10; Gal 1:15; 2:9), but he does not think that it is something restricted to him alone. On the contrary, his communities share in that grace (Phil 1:7).

In short, although grace is an ethereal concept, hard to get a handle on, it is a multifaceted reality that Paul believes is active in the world and especially in the lives of those who follow Jesus Christ. In this sense, grace is both a given and something that we should not hesitate to ask for or to wish upon others.

60. What does Paul mean by the expression "in Christ"?

This is one of Paul's simplest yet most profound expressions. At times Paul uses synonymous phrases such as "in Christ Jesus" or "in the Lord" (Rom 16:3, 22; 1 Thess 3:8). Baptism incorporates one "into Christ" in a totally new fashion. Paul believed that faith dramatically changed an individual. For a person of faith, reality itself is changed. This is more than just a spatial concept. It is not merely moving from one position to another. Paul uses poetic language to describe what, in essence, some see as a mystical union between the believer and Christ. "Thus if one is in Christ, one is a new creation" (2 Cor 5:17 my translation; cf. "in Christ" at Rom 8:1; 2 Cor 12:2, 19). Being incorporated into Christ means becoming totally reborn. By virtue of baptism this action involves dying with Christ, becoming dead to the power of sin, and living an entirely new life "in Christ" (Rom 6:11). Those who live "in Christ" participate in his death and resurrection (Rom 6:8–11). It means surrendering to the power of Christ in such a way that one allows the risen Christ to direct completely his or her life. So dramatically changed is a person that Paul goes so far as to say, "...it is no longer I who live, but it is Christ who lives in me" (Gal 2:20). In essence, it is a mutual indwelling of Christ in the believer and the believer in Christ.

As far as scholars are aware, the expression "in Christ" seems unique to Paul. The Pauline churches are well aware of the vocabulary. At times it refers to the community's new life together in Christ (Rom 12:5; Gal 1:22). At other times Paul uses the expression to affirm that certain individuals have entered this state (Rom 16:7). Theologically, the expression implies the reception of God's grace and the effect of salvation through Jesus Christ. The concept, then, is connected with many other Pauline terms and phrases used to describe the Christ-event. Although it can be considered a formula, its meaning is obviously more profound than a simple label would imply.

61. Why is the cross so important to Paul?

If one were to count importance by the number of occurrences of a word, the cross would be seemingly minor compared to other ideas in Paul. The word is found only six times in the undisputed letters of Paul and is absent from Romans. But the notion of the crucified Christ is of utmost importance to Paul. One scholar even characterizes the cross and all that it means as the major aspect of Paul's spirituality. (See Gorman, *Cruciformity,* in the Recommended Readings.)

Paul is most conscious that his duty is to "proclaim Christ crucified, a stumbling block to Jews and foolishness to Gentiles" (1 Cor 1:23). Paul has a preference for speaking of "Christ crucified" (1 Cor 1:23; 2:2, 8; 2 Cor 13:4; Gal 3:1). The cross is the most paradoxical element in Christian doctrine. From a strictly secular viewpoint, it represents utter defeat. Yet for Christians, the cross represents the greatest victory that can ever be. Paul was keenly aware of this paradox: "For the message about the cross is foolishness to those who are perishing, but to us who are being saved it is the power of God" (1 Cor 1:18). When confronting the

Corinthian community for their divisiveness, Paul intently reminds them that his utmost concern is not to rob the cross of Christ of its true meaning. He is not concerned with preaching eloquently so that people would be persuaded by his erudition (1 Cor 1:17). Nor is he concerned to make the gospel message easy to accept, for in essence it is a difficult message for Jew and Gentile alike. The most important message he can impart is Christ crucified (1 Cor 2:2).

He acknowledges that some of his converts revert to former ways of behavior precisely because they fear being persecuted for the cross of Christ (Gal 6:12). His response is powerful and shows the depth of his devotion to the cross: "But far be it from me to glory except in the cross of our Lord Jesus Christ, by which the world has been crucified to me, and I to the world" (Gal 6:14 RSV). Paul is not ashamed of the image of Christ on the cross, and he does not tolerate those who would hide the fact or run from it (Gal 3:1; 5:11; Phil 2:8; 3:18). In fact, believers are by nature "crucified" along with the Lord (Rom 6:6; Gal 5:24), as Paul proudly asserts that he has been "crucified with Christ" (Gal 2:19; cf. Gal 6:14). At the very depth of our new life in Christ is embracing the cross and surrendering to its power to transform our lives.

In Paul, the cross has a dual message. The primary message is to focus on the sacrifice that Jesus Christ made to become the Savior of the world. He suffered death, even a humiliating death on a cross, so that life might be restored (Phil 2:8–11; 2 Cor 13:4). Yet, for Paul, the cross also represents the call of all disciples of Jesus to embrace total self-giving and heartfelt love of God and neighbor as the heart of the gospel message. Jesus' sacrifice on the cross was unique (1 Cor 1:13) and it was done out of ignorance of the ruling powers at the time (1 Cor 2:8), but followers of Christ allow themselves to be crucified with him so that they might live in the newness of faith (Gal 2:20). Suffering and giving oneself freely to others for the sake of the faith is an act of embracing the cross of Jesus Christ. Ironically, crucifixion is an act of true power that is vindicated by the resurrection (1 Cor 1:17–18, 24; 15:43; cf. 2 Cor 12:9).

This image also resounds in the Pauline tradition where the cross is acknowledged as the means through which reconciliation came to the world (2 Cor 5:17; Eph 2:16; Col 1:20). The cross stands at the center of Paul's message because it is the unique act of God's obedient Son through which he humbled himself in order to bring salvation and redemption into the world. Thus Paul holds the cross firmly before his congregations as both an image of hope and a contradictory sign to emulate.

62. Why is Jesus the "new Adam"? Is Paul the only one who speaks this way?

This is one of the more creative ideas of Paul concerning the significance of Jesus Christ. No other writing of the NT develops this idea, and as far as we know, Paul is the first Christian to have made the comparison between Adam and Christ. It serves as an excellent illustration of how Paul uses OT texts in an innovative way.

The two passages that explicitly treat this subject are found in First Corinthians and Romans (1 Cor 15:22, 45–49; Rom 5:12–14). In Paul's conception of salvation history, a dramatic comparison can be made between Adam and Jesus Christ because, in Christ, God is virtually making a new creation (cf. Gen 2:7). Paul's comparison looks like this:

Adam	*Christ*
first man and human being	last Adam
became a living being	became a life-giving spirit
natural being	spiritual being
earthly being	heavenly being
we bear his earthly image	we bear his heavenly image
brought sin into the world	brought salvation into the world by grace

was disobedient	was obedient
brought death into the world	brought resurrected life into the world
all shall die	all shall have life

One can see from this comparison that Paul has carefully thought out the theological implications of Christ's coming. He views Adam as a "type" (Greek *typos*) of Christ (Rom 5:14). Adam was the prototype of what should have been the ideal human being, but he failed by his transgression of God's law. Christ, however, as the new Adam, succeeds where the original Adam failed. Christ's obedience stands in stark contrast to Adam's disobedience. Thus, eternal life becomes a possibility for all who are modeled after Christ, whereas death is the reality for all modeled after Adam. Paul's use of typology to outline his understanding is a standard ancient interpretive practice. Seeing the world through comparisons such as "types" was a prominent way to adapt scriptural passages to new circumstances.

Paul's image has a profound effect on his theology. It is one of the archetypical explanations of his view of salvation history. Just as God had acted creatively in Adam to bring the family of humankind into existence, so God now acts creatively in the person of Jesus Christ to bring into existence a new family of faithful ones. Some interpreters think that this conception is so prominent that it even influences parts of Paul's letters where Adam is never explicitly mentioned.

The best example of an implicit use of this notion is the famous christological hymn in Philippians (2:6–11). Drawing out the comparison would look like this:

Adam	*Christ*
in the image of God	in the form of God
grasped at equality	did not grasp at equality
puffed himself up	emptied himself
made himself master	made himself a slave

exalted himself	humbled himself
was brought low by God	was raised on high by God

Whether Paul intended the hymn to be read in this fashion is uncertain, but the implicit comparison does resemble Paul's explicit Adam/Christ contrast found in Romans and First Corinthians. The point is that Paul has creatively interpreted the coming of Jesus Christ in a broader theological framework that reconceptualizes salvation history. Christ as the new Adam is a profound image that provides hope for the world.

63. What does Paul mean when he talks about putting on the new man of Christ?

Paul taught that one of the main effects of the Christ-event was that it totally transformed individuals, as well as the world. He believed strongly that Christ's coming, death, and resurrection had a dramatic impact on human existence. The language of "newness" was an inherent part of this change. The notion occurs in Paul's undisputed letters and is also developed in Colossians and Ephesians. Paul thereby contrasts our "old nature" or "old self" with our "new nature" or "new self" (Rom 6:6; Col 3:9–10; Eph 4:22–24). In essence, it is putting on a "new humanity" (*kainon anthrōpon;* Eph 4:24; Col 3:10; NRSV and NAB, "new self"). It also entails casting aside the "works of darkness" and putting on "the armor of light" (Rom 13:12).

Paul associates this change with baptism. Baptism into Christ was the act of clothing oneself with Christ (Gal 3:27). In fact, the expression "taking off" and "putting on" may actually reflect the baptismal practice of the early church. The reference reminds one of the act of dressing and undressing. When the newly initiated emerged from the waters of baptism, having stripped themselves of their ordinary clothes (and the old life), these new believers were clothed in a white garment that signified their new life in Christ. The old self had been crucified with Christ; the new self was reborn. The old self was buried with

Christ; the new self was raised to "walk in the newness of life" (Rom 6:4; a metaphor for living righteously). The practice remains in baptismal rituals of some churches, though frequently the garment is nothing more than a symbolic piece of white cloth. Another aspect of Paul's thought is the connection with the Adam/Christ contrast. Our old self is identified with Adam. Our new self is identified with "the last Adam" who is Christ (1 Cor 15:44–49). The old self is corruptible, but the new self will be incorruptible. The old existence is natural and physical; the new existence is supernatural and spiritual. Paul delights in this contrast and bolsters it by his teaching on the resurrection (see question 72). We lay aside our mortality and "put on" the immortality that comes with new life in Christ (1 Cor 15:53–54). This dramatic change is only possible because of Christ's resurrection, which is our ultimate hope.

Sometimes people wonder about the effect of Paul's teaching. On the one hand, it sounds wonderful. It is hope-filled and energizing. On the other hand, one does not need to look far even within the Christian community to see evidence that this transformation does not seem to have been fully effected. How do we explain this?

We must remember that Paul carefully balances the contrast between the "already" and "not yet" in the Christ-event. Salvation has been achieved, yet not every believer lives at all times in that salvation. There is more to come and more to be achieved. Paul can boldly proclaim this dramatic change as accomplished once and for all in Jesus Christ. However, he also knows that vestiges of the old remain in human existence. Therefore, he regularly exhorts his communities to put their beliefs into action. Living the new life of Christ is as much a challenge today as it was for Paul.

64. Why is Abraham so important to Paul?

It is nearly impossible to overstate the importance of Abraham, but this is true for more than just Paul. Three major world faiths trace their oldest ancestor in faith to Abraham: Judaism, Christianity, and Islam. To some degree, Paul's interest in Abraham is a natural product of his Jewish heritage. Yet Paul employs the figure of Abraham in a specific manner that particularly suits his purpose. That is doubtless where you get the correct impression that Abraham is quite important to Paul's theology. This is expounded primarily in Galatians and Romans and it directly relates to Paul's notion of justification by faith (see question 66).

Let's look briefly at Galatians 3—4. In typical rabbinic fashion, Paul relies upon his understanding of a passage from the OT that refers to God "crediting" Abraham with "righteousness" because of his faith (Gal 3:6; cf. Gen 15:6). Paul is fascinated by Abraham's faith. When God made a covenant with Abraham and promised that he would be the father of many nations, Abraham simply believed God. Thus, for Paul, Abraham is the preeminent OT figure of faith. He is the icon of human responsiveness to God's graciousness. God extended an outstretched hand in covenant, and Abraham accepted it. Paul sees in this simple gesture the most profound meaning of true faith. The Abrahamic covenant is not built upon conforming to the law. It is based upon a relationship extended by God and received by Abraham. More importantly, the fruit of this covenant is God fulfilling the promise through the gift of an heir for Abraham. Paul plays on the OT text by referring to "seed" (singular "descendant" instead of the collective word in Hebrew, "descendants" or "offspring") so that he can show Christ as the fulfillment of God's promise to Abraham (Gal 3:16, 19; cf. Gen 12:7; 15:18).

Paul develops his thought further with an allegory about freedom (Gal 4:21–31). Again in typical rabbinic fashion, he uses the OT story of Abraham's two sons, one by his concubine slave woman Hagar (i.e., Ishmael), and the other by his wife Sarah (i.e., Isaac). Through a somewhat contorted interpretation of the OT texts, Paul contrasts being the child of a slave woman versus being the child of a free woman. In his understanding Christ has set us free from the obligations of the law precisely so that we could live in freedom and not return to enslavement. We are true descendants of Abraham if we live in freedom by faith (cf. Rom 11:1; 2 Cor 11:22).

In Romans Paul reiterates and expands his thoughts on Abraham (Rom 4:1–25; 9:6–13). Paul explains that God credited righteousness to Abraham, not as something owed him for services he had rendered, but as a gift from God. Abraham was thus no employee but a recipient of God's favor. God's promise was fulfilled to Abraham in that he did, in fact, become "the father of many nations" (Gen 17:4–8). Paul's mission to the Gentiles is rooted in this OT promise that has now gone beyond Abraham to Christ (see Isa 40–55).

65. Why does Paul have so much to say about circumcision?

Circumcision was tied explicitly to Abraham. It was a major concern for Paul for both religious and cultural reasons. Religiously, Paul was a Jew and proud of it. Male circumcision was a prominent aspect of Judaism. It was a key factor for Jewish identity. Self-identity as a Jew was bound up with adherence to God's covenant with Abraham that was to be signed by the act of circumcision (Gen 17:10–12). In Paul's day, circumcision was a standard part of adherence to the Mosaic law, the torah. Jesus was circumcised (Luke 2:21), as was Paul (Phil 3:5).

Once the admission of the Gentiles to the Christian family became an issue, the practice of circumcision took on new importance. There had regularly been Gentiles who were attracted to Judaism because of the strong commitment to an ethical code found in the Torah and the other scriptures. Many of these would-be converts, however, drew a line when they were required to be circumcised. A special group of Gentile converts, who adhered to most of the other expectations of Judaism except circumcision, arose. They were known as Godfearers (Acts 10:2, 22, 35; 13:16,

26). Early in Paul's career, after his conversion/call, he obviously developed second thoughts about the requirement of circumcision. He was not the only one to do so, and we can only speculate what influences provoked a change in policy. Both Acts and Paul agree that the early church decided to eliminate mandatory circumcision as a prerequisite for becoming a disciple of Jesus. It was no longer essential to Christian identity.

Cultural aspects also influenced the situation. In the Hellenistic world secular Greek society scorned circumcision as mutilation of the human body. Moreover, the Hellenistic world established the institution known as the gymnasium, where male athletes competed in the nude (Greek *gymnos* = naked). When Jews living in the diaspora came into contact with gymnasiums, some of them inevitably became sensitive about the visible mark of circumcision that made them easily identifiable. Within Judaism itself circumcision became a topic of discussion. Some Jewish men even went so far as to try to erase the mark of their circumcision by having an operation to reattach their foreskins. Other Jews condemned such a practice as an utter denial of Jewish identity.

Paul's attitude toward circumcision is not simplistic. Paul commends circumcision, provided it does not oppose that which is truly essential in faith; but he simultaneously minimizes it. Physical circumcision, he states explicitly, is of no importance (Rom 2:25—3:1), but neither should one seek to remove one's circumcision. Note the following two texts:

> For a person is not a Jew who is one outwardly, nor is true circumcision something external and physical. Rather, a person is a Jew who is one inwardly, and real circumcision is a matter of the heart—it is spiritual and not literal. Such a person receives praise not from others but from God. (Rom 2:28–29)

> Was anyone at the time of his call already circumcised? Let him not seek to remove the marks of circumcision. Was anyone at the time of his call uncircumcised? Let him not seek

circumcision. Circumcision is nothing, and uncircumcision is nothing; but obeying the commandments of God is everything. (1 Cor 7:18–19)

In the end, for Paul, what is important is the interior attitude one has toward God and God's law (Gal 5:6).

66. What does Paul mean by "justification by faith"? Don't Catholics and Protestants view this teaching differently?

You are right in suggesting that traditionally there was a different approach used by Catholics and Protestants to understand the notion of justification by faith. But this difference is more due to complex historical factors dating from the time of the Reformation (sixteenth century) than from Paul. First, let me get at your question by briefly describing Paul's understanding.

The Greek word for justification (*dikaiosis;* and the verb *dikaioun*) is closely related to the word for "righteousness" *(dikaiosynē).* In the OT when the word for righteousness was used, it generally meant "right living" or a morally upright life lived before the eyes of God. When Paul used the concept and applied it to Christian faith, however, he employed Abraham as his primary model. Using the story from Genesis about Abraham's call to faith in God (Gen 15:6), Paul emphasized not Abraham's moral uprightness, but the freedom with which he accepted God's mysterious call without question (Rom 4:2–3). God pronounced Abraham righteous because of his obedience. In typical rabbinic fashion, Paul used the OT expression that God credited righteousness to Abraham to summarize what he understood by faith. Faith—that is, absolute trust in God despite not knowing where God will lead you—is a gift freely given. One does not earn it, nor can one buy it. Paul believed that in Jesus Christ humankind had been given the ultimate gift of God, being justified freely by faith. What was necessary was a free response to this gift, namely, a life lived as though we were already saved by God's grace.

So can we succinctly define justification? Many scholars have come up with definitions that I think contain the most essential elements (e.g., J. D. G. Dunn, N. T. Wright, and M. J. Gorman in the Recommended Readings). *Justification is God's restoration in Christ Jesus of a covenantal relationship that now enables people to love God and their neighbor freely while awaiting final vindication on the day of judgment.* Justification means that we do not act out our love of God and neighbor out of fear but out of faith. We are confident that salvation has already been achieved in Christ Jesus but that, by our lives of loving service, we live in hope of a future kingdom where God's final vindication awaits us.

At the time of the Reformation, many people in the Catholic Church had diverged considerably from this understanding of justification by faith. In the selling of indulgences and other practices, Martin Luther and others discerned the corruption of Paul's insight. It looked as if Catholics believed they earned salvation by good deeds or, worse, by buying salvation in parcels. In reality, both Protestants and Catholics caricatured one another over their understanding. Catholics emphasized good works, the sacraments, the church, while Protestants emphasized faith alone, the Bible as God's Word, and the individual decision to follow Christ. Fortunately, at the end of the twentieth century, dialogue between Protestants and Catholics breached some of this misunderstanding. Lutherans and Catholics have issued a common declaration that clarifies and moves beyond this disagreement (see question 67). Although there are still differences of approach and interpretation, both parties can agree that Paul taught that justification by faith implies God's free gift of salvation that has come in Jesus Christ.

67. Don't people also have to do good works to be saved?

This is precisely the kind of language that has been problematic historically. It implies that we earn salvation by doing good deeds, rather than by receiving salvation as a gift that God has given us in Jesus Christ. This position does not mean that there is no role for good works. On the contrary, good works, or a righteous life, flow from the salvation that has already been achieved by Jesus' death and resurrection. If Paul had thought an ethically righteous life was unimportant, he would scarcely have devoted large sections of his letters to ethical issues. The crux of the matter, however, is which comes first—good deeds or justification by faith. Good deeds flow from faith, not the other way around. Yet if one does not live the Christian life righteously, then one's faith would be hollow. More accurately, however, one must go a step further: Faith and action both proceed from God's grace. Faith and action belong together, but grace comes first.

We might take some comfort in knowing that Paul's teaching on faith must have caused some misunderstanding already in early Christianity. The Letter of James reflects a discussion about the interrelationship between faith and good works that probably arose from a misunderstanding or misapplication of Paul's ideas (Jas 2:14–26). James argues that faith must be accompanied by good works not because they earn salvation but because they go hand in hand with what God has given and has demanded. He says,

> So faith by itself, if it has no works, is dead. But some one will say, "You have faith and I have works." Show me your faith apart from your works, and I by my works will show you my faith. (Jas 2:17–18 RSV)

We should not pit James against Paul on this question. Both would be misunderstood if we thought they argued mutually exclusive positions. Rather, faith ultimately leads one to a righteous life and, conversely, one's righteous deeds indicate that faith truly resides in the one whose actions are rooted in love. As Paul himself says, "For in Christ Jesus neither circumcision nor uncircumcision counts for anything; the only thing that counts is faith working *(energoumenē)* through love" (Gal 5:6).

The traditional dichotomy between an exaggerated Catholic and Protestant tradition on this question, fortunately, has been addressed by formal ecumenical dialogue. On October 31, 1999 (Reformation Day), Lutherans and Catholics signed an agreement in Augsburg, Germany, that outlined a mutual understanding of this topic. This "Joint Declaration on the Doctrine of Justification" contains forty-four common declarations that have finally laid to rest the gap created more than four hundred years ago by the Protestant Reformation and the subsequent Counter-Reformation. Pope John Paul II expressed some cautions about a few concepts that will require further dialogue and clarification but, nevertheless, agreed to its publication as a common expression of faith between the two communions. It will take many years to bridge this chasm especially at a popular level, but contemporary biblical scholarship has helped enormously to put Paul's teaching in perspective.

68. What was Paul's attitude toward the law? Doesn't he contradict himself on the law at times?

This is one of the most complex theological topics in Paul. We have noted before that Paul was not a systematic thinker. He was not attempting to collect his ideas into a comprehensive digest of his thought. We should not be surprised, then, to find that his reflections on the law are at times confusing, and seemingly contradictory. Moreover, in recent years there has been a reevaluation of Paul's notion of the law that has led to a "new perspective" (see question 69).

The background of your question is again primarily located in the OT. The law or torah was the primary defining characteristic of Judaism. It was God's holy instruction. It revealed what was and was not permitted in the arena of human behavior. Paul's understanding of the law is scattered throughout his letters, but in a few instances he talks at length about the law and provides a summary of his thoughts. I will try to synthesize

Paul's ideas, especially as they are found in Galatians 3 and 5 and Romans 2—4 and 7.

On the one hand, Paul has a positive estimation of the law. It was God's gift to the Jews in order to help them know God's will and put it into action (Rom 2:17–18). It was not meant to become a burden but a yardstick, a way of measuring one's life in accord with God's expectations. For a time the law functioned as a disciplinarian (Gal 3:24–25 NAB and NRSV; RSV "custodian"). Its purpose was to supervise human conduct much as a tutor oversees the behavior of children. It was a means to make people conscious of sinfulness (Rom 3:20; 7:7). Paul does not believe that the law was intended only in literal fashion and that it demanded external conformity. He admits that there is a prior internal dimension that takes precedence (Rom 2:27–28). The law was meant not only to be heard or learned by rote, but also to be put into action (Rom 2:13). He counts himself among those who were zealous for the law (Phil 3:5–6), and he considers the law "holy" (Rom 7:12).

On the other hand, Paul recognizes serious limitations of the law. The law can lead to a legalistic mentality and can become a barrier, rather than an aid, to righteousness in God's eyes. He is careful to avoid equating the law with sinfulness (Rom 7:7), but the law did not fulfill its goal properly. That is why there was a need for another means of salvation. For a time the law functioned properly in enabling Israel to live out God's commands, but then, instead of diminishing sinfulness, it increased it. Rather than giving the Jews an advantage for righteous living, the law ended up being a liability. It increased the violations of the law, a development that paradoxically allowed grace to increase (Rom 5:20), that is, in the person of Jesus Christ.

In the end, the law was only a temporary fix on a more persistent problem of human sinfulness. What was needed was not a new law but an entirely new way of living according to God's grace. Paul believes that this is exactly what was achieved in Jesus Christ. His coming made the law no longer necessary. Yet Paul does not conceive that the law has been overthrown by Jesus.

Paradoxically Jesus upholds the law because he alone has the ability to live the law to its fullest extent. Jesus Christ, as God's Son, accomplished what no human being could—fulfill the law. And those who live in Christ also fulfill the law by loving others in a Christ-like fashion (Rom 13:8–10; Gal 5:13–14).

So is Paul's attitude toward the law a contradiction? If it only applied to Jews, one might suggest that. But, as some scholars have suggested, the apparent contradiction is mitigated considerably if we recognize that Paul's main concern with the law is how it applies now to the Gentiles as well as the Jews. Now that Christ has come, and Gentiles have embraced him along with the Jews, the law no longer functions as it did formerly.

69. What is meant by the "new perspective" on Paul?

The term stems from the groundbreaking work of E. P. Sanders (*Paul and Palestinian Judaism* [Philadelphia: Fortress, 1977]), though J. D. G. Dunn first coined the term and applied it to this phenomenon (see the Recommended Readings). Essentially, the work of Sanders delivered a decisive correction to the heretofore common characterization of Judaism as a strictly legalistic religion, as compared with the "gospel" orientation of Christianity. This led to a further contrast between "works-righteousness" and "grace-justification," slavery to the law and the freedom derived from the gospel, and so on. It is no exaggeration to say that this sharp contrast between law and gospel has reigned supreme since the time of Martin Luther and has become the hallmark of most understandings of Paul's thought on this matter.

In brief one can explain the "new perspective" as follows. Judaism was not actually a legalistic religion at all. Rather, according to Sanders, who built upon the work of earlier scholars, Judaism was a religion of "covenantal nomism." This means that belonging to the chosen people was not something achieved by adherence to the law (torah) but by belonging to God's people through the covenant. This status was God's gift;

it could not be earned. However, remaining properly tied to the covenant required adherence to the stipulations of the law. Obedience to God's law, then, was not a neatly arranged legalism but a living out of one's identity bestowed through the covenant.

Based on this perspective, Paul must be understood as not denigrating doing works of the law self-righteously to earn salvation. Instead, Paul's teaching about the law is directed to the practical lived experience of maintaining the right relationship with God envisioned in the covenant. It has to do with ethnic identity as a member of the covenant. Sanders acknowledges that Paul is not entirely consistent on what he says about the law. As we have said before, Paul was not a systematic thinker. He wrote letters that addressed diverse situations and circumstances that required varied responses. Nonetheless, this "new perspective" provides a long-needed corrective both to how Christians have viewed Judaism and how we have understood Paul's seeming contradictions on the question of the law.

This scholarly work has had a far-reaching effect. No Pauline scholar can choose to ignore its implications. As in the case of other scholarly findings that show first-century Judaism to be quite complex and not monolithic, so this new outlook points out the weaknesses of earlier views of the Jewish law. One good byproduct of this discussion is indeed an improved possibility for Jewish-Christian dialogue.

There are, however, scholars who are already calling for a "newer perspective," one that does not overlook Paul's call to adhere to the law in some regards, even if the transformation achieved in Jesus Christ requires a shift in how one leads a righteous life (e.g., A. Andrew Das, *Paul, the Law, and the Covenant* [Peabody, MA: Hendrickson, 2001]). This scholarly conversation might be upsetting (let alone confusing) to some who want a definitive answer to Paul's view of the law. I suggest, rather, that the ongoing discussion of this recurring topic is a boon to all who struggle to understand Paul on his own terms. Part of the charm of the sacred scriptures is exactly that each generation wrestles with them and thereby gains new insight that might just make a difference for succeeding generations.

70. What does Paul mean by the expression, "Christ is the end of the law"?

This important expression in Romans 10:4 requires careful consideration. Whole books have been written about it. The key word to understand is "end"; what does it mean? The Greek word *telos* can have two senses. One meaning is the termination or finality of something. In this case, Paul would be saying that the coming of Jesus Christ has done away with the law. It is over, it no longer has a function, and it has been superseded. The other meaning of the word, however, is "goal-oriented" or something that strives to attain its fullness. In this case, Paul could mean that the law was pointing toward Christ all along as the one who could bring it to completion, to its fullness. There is no way to resolve the absolute tension of these two meanings on the grounds of grammar or syntax alone. Paul possibly had both senses of the phrase in mind when he insisted that "Christ is the end of the law, so that everyone who believes may be justified" (Rom 10:4 my translation).

What I think is most important is not to overlook that, even if Paul understands that the law no longer exercises the same authority for Christians that it once had for Jews, Christians' lives will not contradict the essentials of the law. For example, in the context of serious divisions and infighting, Paul can insist to the Galatians: "the whole law is summed up in a single commandment, 'You shall love your neighbor as yourself'" (Gal 5:14), a comment reminiscent of Jesus' own teaching based upon parts of the law (Matt 22:39; Luke 10:27). If Paul thinks of Christ as the end of the law, it is because Christ's message goes far beyond what the law demanded.

71. I get confused by some terms that Paul uses like salvation, redemption, justification, glorification, and exaltation. Aren't they all basically the same thing?

I can understand your confusion. It is not easy to keep all these concepts straight, and there is in fact some overlap in the various terms that are found in the Pauline letters. Yet there are sufficient distinctions that can be made validly. To simplify matters, I will try to define rather succinctly each of the terms in your question, as well as some other related terms found in the Pauline corpus. But first, let's review Paul's basic theological stance.

At the heart of Paul's thought is the conviction that Jesus Christ is the primary vehicle for God's definitive gracious actions toward humanity. Sometimes scholars use the (admittedly vague) term, the "Christ-event." This all-embracing concept, however, has multiple facets to it. Because he is not writing as a theologian, Paul is not always as clear as one would like on the various layers of this Christ-event. Thus the language gets jumbled a bit. In a sense, Paul employs certain terms as metaphors to describe this complex reality. He is nonetheless clear that the coming of Jesus Christ has accomplished certain realities that can be described, and that is why a variety of terminology arises.

The effects of the Christ-event are understood as: justification, salvation, and redemption. These are supplemented by sanctification, exaltation, glorification, and reconciliation. Some of these terms are addressed in other questions (e.g., questions 58, 66, and 94), but here the task is to interrelate them. There is, in my judgment, no singular word that embraces all of these concepts. Thus it is difficult to say which is primary and which is secondary.

Measured simply by the sheer quantity of references in the letters, *justification* is the primary concept (question 66). As we saw, it is God's action—through Christ—of making human beings "righteous" in God's eyes. Because it is intimately tied to faith (the personal relationship of the believer with Christ), justification is obviously a primary result of the Christ-event.

Salvation is also very important in Paul. This term might be most familiar because all Christians associate Jesus Christ's life and death with salvation from sin. It also has a long and venerable OT background that presents God as the ultimate Savior who extends salvation to Israel (Isa 45:15; Zech 8:7). Interestingly, Paul only once calls Jesus "Savior" (Greek *sōtēr;* Phil 3:20, but see also Eph 5:23), although he frequently uses salvation terminology as a primary effect. Typically, Paul asserts that though we have already been saved from sin and its evil effects by God's gracious action in Jesus Christ, the fullness of salvation awaits the final coming of God's kingdom (cf. Rom 13:11 and 2 Cor 6:2; 1 Thess 5:8).

Redemption is obviously a related term, but it originates from the notion of "buying" someone back. It can often refer to "redeeming" someone from slavery or bondage, as God did the Israelites (e.g., Isa 43:14; Ps 78:35) or a master does to a slave (Exod 21:30). For Paul, God's action in Christ is a generous act of redemption. God has bought us back with his own Son. Jesus paid the ultimate price (death on a cross), with our freedom as the result. Though he never calls Jesus "redeemer," he does label him our "redemption" (1 Cor 1:30; cf. Rom 3:24). Indeed, in that same passage in First Corinthians Paul strings several terms together to speak of Christ: wisdom, righteousness, sanctification, redemption.

Sanctification is yet another result of Christ's action. This term is more closely associated with the activity of the Holy Spirit (Rom 15:16) but also comes from Jesus Christ (1 Cor 1:2). The root idea of sanctification is, of course, becoming God-like (i.e., holy). Only God is holy, but we are made derivatively holy by Christ's action. For Paul, sanctification is another result of the Christ-event, but it comes after salvation and justification (Rom 6:19, 22). It is deemed an advantage that leads one toward eternal life (Rom 6:20–23). Because sanctification has already come in Christ, the community of believers appropriately can be called "the saints" (Rom 1:7; 1 Cor 1:2; etc.), even though sanctification will not be ultimately fulfilled until we reside with God in the kingdom.

Exaltation and *glorification* are interrelated terms. They are connected to Christ's Lordship by virtue of his victory over sin and death on the cross. God has exalted Christ in the resurrection (Phil 2:9). He is enthroned on high at the right hand of God (Rom 8:34). Indeed one could say that exaltation is an all-encompassing term for the resurrection, ascension to glory, and enthronement of Christ. It is God's vindication of Jesus as his Son (Rom 1:4). Glorification is related by virtue of the focus on the heavenly dwelling of Christ after his resurrection. In the OT, "glory" is one of the most dazzling aspects of God, connected with God's Lordship over creation (Exod 24:17; Ps 19:1). Christ now shares in that glorification (2 Cor 3:18; Phil 2:9–10). One other aspect of this dimension of Christ is that it is also our destiny. We who share in Christ's life by faith are also destined to be glorified (cf. Rom 8:29–30). In typically Pauline fashion, it is both now and yet to come. Those who are justified are already glorified (Rom 8:30), yet we await the full transformation into glory (1 Cor 15:43–44; Phil 3:20).

Now, having outlined descriptions of these expressions, we can see that they are not exactly the same thing but that they are closely related. There is some precedence in the list. Justification and salvation precede sanctification and glorification, but one should not press the distinctions too hard. As Paul himself notes:

> For those whom he foreknew he also predestined to be conformed to the image of his Son, in order that he might be the firstborn within a large family. And those whom he predestined he also called; and those whom he called he also justified; and those whom he justified he also glorified. (Rom 8:29–30)

All of these actions are the result of God's graciousness toward humanity.

72. What does Paul say about resurrection?

Resurrection theology is a key element in Paul's thought. It is, of course, a central concept in Christian faith, so it is not surprising to find it discussed by Paul. In a sense, the resurrection of Jesus, and the promise of our own resurrection from the dead, undergird everything we believe. Paul speaks of resurrection throughout his letters (except Second Thessalonians, Titus, and Philemon), but the most extensive treatment of it is in First Corinthians (chap. 15). He begins by reminding the Corinthians of the gospel message he preached. It was already for Paul a traditional message, one he had received and then passed on (vv. 1, 3–11). The traditional message included the following sequence: Christ died, was buried, was raised on the third day, and appeared to a series of groups and individuals, the last of whom was Paul himself (vv. 3–8). He also refined the message somewhat, adding references to the fulfillment of scripture (vv. 3, 4).

Note that Paul never describes the resurrection of Jesus in detail. Certainly he understands it as a physical and historical reality. Yet as an "apocalyptic" event, it lies beyond history. The vocabulary of resurrection (especially, Greek *egeirō*) is often in the passive voice ("was raised"), indicating that God's power accomplishes this reality. For Paul, Jesus is the "firstfruits" of the resurrection (v. 20), the one who is the "firstborn" in the new community of faith (Rom 8:29). His resurrection is our insurance and assurance that we, too, will be raised. Jesus Christ now intercedes for us with God and will see that we attain the final promise of resurrection (Rom 8:34). Paul goes so far as to make belief in the resurrection of Jesus an essential element of true confessional faith (Rom 10:9).

This message, however, had not been effective for everyone in the community at Corinth. Paul goes on to challenge those who are denying the resurrection of the dead (v. 12). Using very strong language, Paul asserts that faith would be in vain or empty if the resurrection were a fraud (vv. 13–19; see 1 Thess 4:13–18 where Paul tackles a similar issue). The final extended section of the chapter outlines some of Paul's thoughts on the practical questions that concern the Corinthians: How will the resurrection take place (vv. 35–58)? At the center of Paul's explanation is a contrast between that which is earthly and that which is heavenly. He uses contrasting terms like "natural body" and "spiritual body," "earthly body" and "heavenly body," and "corruptible" and "incorruptible." Resurrected life, as Paul understands it, is a mystery (v. 51), yet it can be described to some degree. It is a transformation and an experience of exaltation. Using stock OT apocalyptic imagery (Joel 2:1–2; Zech 9:14), Paul speaks of the instantaneous metamorphosis that will come upon believers when the resurrection of the dead takes place (vv. 51–53). He also affirms that the resurrection was God's vindication of Jesus, which will also be our fate. Sharing Christ's sufferings means we will also share in the resurrection (Phil 3:10–11).

In sum, Paul's understanding of resurrection is rich and complex. He is not preoccupied with describing it. He asserts it as a fundamental of Christian faith and a essential component of Christian hope that God ultimately has the power to transform this corruptible body into an incorruptible one.

73. What does Paul mean when he calls us "adopted children of God"?

As far as scholars can determine, Paul is the first to utilize the notion of "adoption" in a theological context. The word (Greek *hyiothesia*) does not occur elsewhere in the NT. Nowhere does Paul define it as such, but he uses the expression in several different passages that give a hint as to how he views it (Rom 8:15, 23; 9:4; Gal 4:5).

We first notice that the background of the term is likely to be found in the OT. Paul was familiar with the Davidic covenant. When God made a covenant with David, he received him as his adopted son (2 Sam 7:14). In other words, the king entered into a relationship with God not as a natural son or legitimate heir, but as one who has been adopted into a legitimate line of heirs. Paul extends this notion to Christians who thereby become adopted children of God (Gal 4:4–5; Rom 8:15, 23). He contrasts this legitimate adoption with being a slave. Christians are not called to slavery (to sin, to death) but to freedom (in the Christian life). This adoption, accomplished by God's grace at work in Jesus Christ, allows us to cry out "Abba, Father," as true "children of God" (Gal 4:6; Rom 8:15). For Paul, then, adoption is another aspect of God's gracious action toward humanity. It is the way by which we are given a special relationship with God that transforms our lives. The Spirit of God facilitates this adoption process so that we can inherit the promises God made to Abraham, which are now fulfilled in Christ.

Paul also adds a future dimension to this notion. He associates adoption with the future fullness of redemption that will be accomplished when God's plan comes to full fruition (Rom 8:23; cf. Eph 1:5). Adoption is consequently both a past reality and a future hope.

74. Doesn't Paul say somewhere that you have to be baptized to be saved?

There is no passage in Paul that clearly states that baptism is essential. Paul's teaching about baptism is multifaceted. There is no doubt that baptism was important for Paul, but interpretations can vary as to what Paul actually meant by baptism. Pentecostal and charismatic communions, for instance, associate baptism with "baptism in the Holy Spirit" rather than with the ritual of water baptism. Since the earliest days of Christian faith, the church has practiced baptism. Indeed, there are pre-Christian roots to baptism (i.e., ritual washing) as evidenced in Jewish communities such as Qumran and the practice of John the Baptist (Mark 1:4–8). Jesus was baptized (Matt 3:16; Mark 1:9) and so was Paul (Acts 9:18). He also admits to having baptized in his ministry (1 Cor 1:14–16), but denies that baptism is the major thrust of his apostolic work (1 Cor 1:17).

Yet Paul refers to baptism in several important ways. It reflects an early stage of baptismal theology in which some aspects had not yet been crystallized. For instance, in Paul baptism is most often described as baptism "into Christ" (Gal 3:27; Rom 6:3) rather than in the later trinitarian formula (Matt 28:19) or the earlier Christian formulation, "baptism in the name of Jesus" (Acts 2:38; 10:48). Some Christians in the Evangelical tradition deny that the ritual of baptism is necessary for salvation. Based on their reading of Romans 10:9–13, they think it is sufficient to confess that "Jesus is Lord." What is important for them is enunciating faith in Jesus Christ, accepting him as one's personal Lord and Savior. It must be admitted, however, that Paul refers frequently enough to baptism to hold that it was an essential part of the believer's journey of faith. Baptism is the way in which one dies with Christ in order to be raised with him (Rom 6:3–4). Baptism changes one so fundamentally that a new relationship is created. The baptized now "belongs" to Christ (thus the implication of 1 Cor 1:12–16; cf. 1 Cor 15:23). Baptism creates a deep union with Christ and brings one into contact with a new community, the "body of Christ" (1 Cor 12:13, 27). Baptism incorporates one into this communion of "saints" who are called to live virtuous lives because they have received God's gracious gift of salvation (1 Thess 4:1–7; Rom 6:1–11). In short, Paul's views on baptism are consistent with later developments in theology and are part of his overarching perspective.

75. Does Paul speak of any other sacraments besides baptism?

One must keep in mind that speaking of "sacraments" in the Pauline letters is anachronistic. The letters were written before the church had formally delineated the seven "sacraments" as we have come to know them. Nonetheless, they contain references to rituals that clearly are precursors of our sacraments.

The only extended reference is to the Eucharist. Paul speaks of the "Lord's supper" in First Corinthians (1 Cor 11:17–34). This is an early reference to what the church would later designate the sacrament of the Eucharist. Although Paul nowhere describes specifically who presided at this celebration and exactly how the ritual was conducted, the account gives intriguing hints. Paul says he is responding to the divisions at Corinth about which he has heard and which have affected even the way they celebrate the Lord's Supper. Some have been conducting the ritual as regular meals, rather than as ritual meals. Certain individuals have gotten drunk at them. Others have selfishly eaten ahead of some of the group. And some have been using the eucharistic gatherings to sate their appetites rather than to join the community in prayer (1 Cor 11:18–22). Paul reprimands them. He then recalls the tradition that he had received and consequently passed on to them about the Lord's Supper (1 Cor 11:23–26). This is the oldest account of the Last Supper in the NT. It has affinities to Luke's account (Luke 22:14–20) but differs somewhat from Mark and Matthew's accounts (Mark 14:22–25; Matt 26:26–29).

There is little doubt that what Paul describes is the liturgical ritual that was celebrated in his house churches. In the context of First Corinthians, Paul particularly emphasizes the unifying aspect of the Eucharist. The community disgraces this eucharistic unity when they persist in their own divisions or selfishly feed themselves and neglect the poor. According to Paul, Jesus identified himself with bread and "the cup" as gestures of self-giving for the life of the community. They repeat these actions in memory of Jesus, who identified the cup as a "new covenant" in his own blood (1 Cor 11:25). The community gathers regularly to remember this sacrificial action in confidence that one day the Lord will come again. It expresses an eschatological hope that has yet to be fulfilled. The Eucharist is therefore as much forward-looking as it is a remembrance. Paul also warns the Corinthians that their selfishness will lead to judgment if they do not mend their ways (1 Cor 11:29).

Catholics, in particular, have also taken a passage in Paul as a reference to the sacrament of reconciliation (2 Cor 5:11–21). In the context of his insistence that being "in Christ" changes all reality, Paul voices the confidence that God has reconciled the world to himself by the Christ-event. Our sinfulness is not held against us. It is healed in Christ. Reconciliation is a gift that flows out of the sacrifice that Jesus himself made (Rom 5:10–11). This, in turn, leads to a formal ministry of reconciliation. Paul calls himself and his coworkers "ambassadors for Christ" (v. 20; the plural probably includes Timothy, who is noted as a co-sender in 2 Cor 1:1). They are instruments who carry out Christ's ministry of reconciliation.

Catholics find yet another reference to a sacrament in the Deutero-Pauline epistles of First and Second Timothy (1 Tim 4:14; 2 Tim 1:6). This time the focus is on the sacrament of holy orders. The larger context of the Pastorals is, of course, Paul purportedly giving sage advice to his younger colleagues, Timothy and Titus, on how to function in ministry. These two passages make reference to the "laying on of hands." This was an ancient gesture of passing on authority to someone in the community. It is preserved during contemporary ordination rituals in many churches. The undisputed Pauline letters do not mention the gesture explicitly, but it is mentioned elsewhere in the Bible (Num 27:18–23; Deut 34:9; Acts 6:6; 13:3). Scholars agree, however, that the Pauline letters do not describe an ordination ritual as such. These passages contain the rudimentary elements that shaped the sacramental life of the church at later stages.

76. What about the fate of Israel in Paul's thought?

Paul's teaching about the place of Israel within the Christian framework is perplexing. He tackles the problem head on in Romans 9—11. (For a fine extended treatment of this passage, see Harrington, *Paul on the Mystery of Israel,* in the Recommended Readings.) The crux of the problem is how to incorporate

Israel into salvation as the chosen people if, in fact, they do not accept Jesus Christ as Lord and Savior.

We have pointed out before that Paul is proud of his Jewish heritage. His Christian beliefs did not force him to jettison his entire Jewish background. On the contrary, he incorporated much of it in his theology. The problem was how to understand Israel's status as God's chosen and beloved people once they rejected Jesus and, paradoxically, the Gentiles accepted him. This was all the more urgent for Paul who saw himself as "the apostle to the Gentiles" (Rom 11:13; cf. Rom 1:5; Gal 2:8). Since Paul's explanation of this situation is somewhat convoluted, I will try to summarize it in five basic points that undergird his position.

(1) Paul accepts Israel's status as the chosen people and "the children of the promise" (Rom 9:8) in an irrevocable manner. Their heritage, through the patriarchs and especially Abraham, cannot be revoked. By welcoming the Gentiles God has not rejected his own people (Rom 11:1).

(2) As the prophets pointed out, throughout its history Israel was frequently disobedient to God (Rom 9:25–29; 10:21). God's Word to them did not fail; they failed on their own accord (Rom 9:6). They regularly "stumbled" (Rom 9:32–33), and they did not always attain the adherence to the torah that God intended (Rom 9:31).

(3) Paul then employs the lovely image of an olive tree. In a paradox of faith the Gentiles accepted God's outreach of salvation through Jesus Christ and became "grafted" onto the original tree (Rom 11:13–24). This was not accomplished through the Gentiles' inherent righteousness but through God's grace. The purpose of this reality is to make Israel—God's own chosen people—"jealous" (Rom 11:14). When they see the success of the Gentiles they, too, will want to be saved in the end. They will ultimately be "re-grafted" onto the tree that was their origin (Rom 11:24).

(4) There is not really an ultimate distinction between Jew and Gentile because God calls all to life, brings them into existence, and wills to bring them all to salvation (Rom 10:12–13).

There is no room for haughtiness on either party's side, for all have been disobedient so that all could, in the end, receive God's mercy (Rom 11:32; cf. 2:1–11). When Israel comes to its senses in light of the Gentile success, they will also be saved (Rom 11:26). Since Christ is the "end of the law" (Rom 10:4), the law cannot bring people to salvation. Rather, confessing Jesus as Lord leads to salvation (Rom 10:9–10)

(5) Finally, Paul invokes the "mystery" (Rom 11:25) of salvation in Jesus Christ and attributes it to the incredible goodness of God. Israel can be included in salvation because God promised it, wills it, and can accomplish it. At the conclusion of his argument, so overcome is Paul by the graciousness of God's action, that he erupts in a prayer that begins thus: "O the depth of the riches and wisdom and knowledge of God! How unsearchable are his judgments and how inscrutable his ways!" (Rom 11:33–36).

Some might object that this is too simplistic a summary, but it does contain the basic elements of Paul's position. Paul was convinced that God's grace could accommodate even the stubbornness of his own people, Israel. Modern Christians continue to wrestle with just how God's gracious action of salvation can encompass even those who do not accept Jesus as Lord and Savior.

77. Can you describe Paul's "spirituality"?

Spirituality is an extremely broad topic. In a sense one could designate all of Paul's thought under the category of spirituality. It is virtually a spiritual system, an all-encompassing way of viewing and interpreting God's action in Jesus Christ. I assume, however, that your question presumes a more narrow perspective on spirituality. You are probably interested more in what Paul recommends as avenues to an authentic spiritual life: What does he say about prayer, openness to the Holy Spirit, and the like? Let me summarize what I think are eight key elements of Paul's spirituality.

(1) Most foundational for Paul is a stress on a personal and intimate relationship with God and with the risen Lord Jesus.

Being "in Christ" (question 60) is central to the spiritual life. His own call rested upon this foundation (1 Cor 15:8–9; Gal 1:12). This relationship results in becoming part of a "new creation" (2 Cor 5:17; Gal 6:15). The Holy Spirit seals this relationship and empowers the believer for mission in the world (Rom 8:1–27; 15:19; 1 Thess 1:5–6).

(2) Paul also held an uncompromising faith that God would be (and is) victorious over evil, sin, and death. Nothing can defeat the power of God, no matter how great the obstacles seem in our experience (Rom 8:31–39). He offers the resurrection of Jesus as a kind of "proof" that this is so (1 Cor 15). Jesus was raised and so shall we be. Jesus was victorious and so shall we be. He urged his congregations to hold on to that hope.

(3) Paul was not naive about the necessity of suffering for the sake of the gospel of Jesus Christ and for the sake of the truth. His message was the cross of Jesus Christ, and Christians must always be prepared to be imprinted with this cross (1 Cor 1:17–25). It represents a call to suffering and to self-sacrificial love. Apostleship entails hardships that cannot be avoided. Paul displays them almost as a badge of courage. Paradoxically, he says, this apparent weakness is actually strength (2 Cor 11:21–29; 12:10).

(4) Paul frequently interweaves the three virtues faith, hope, and love into his spiritual perspective. Spirituality involves leading a virtuous life, and these three Christian virtues are the essential ones. At times he emphasizes one or another (e.g., hope is given precedence in 1 Thess), but he concludes that love is superior and conquers all (1 Cor 13:13). In all the paraenetic sections of his letters, he shows that spirituality is intimately tied to ethics. Spirituality is not a retreat from this world, but a living out of the values of the world to come right here and now in this world. He thus encourages attention to the poor and the needy (1 Cor 11:17–34; 2 Cor 9:6–15) as well as other ethical exhortations.

(5) Not surprisingly, Paul also commends prayer as an essential component of the spiritual life. He goes so far as to say we should pray "without ceasing" (1 Thess 5:17; cf. 3:10). He

offers prayers for others (Phil 1:9) and is not shy about asking others to pray for him (Rom 15:30; 1 Thess 5:25). He encourages and offers prayers of thanksgiving as well (2 Cor 9:11–15). He also acknowledges that God, through the Holy Spirit, offers prayerful intercessions and helps us to pray even when we are unable to do so properly (Rom 8:26).

(6) Closely related to prayer is the celebration of sacramental life. In particular, baptism and Eucharist are standard components of Christian life (Gal 3:26–27; 1 Cor 11:17–34).

(7) An underlying assumption of Pauline spirituality is that it is not merely an individual reality; it is lived in a community of faith. Paul emphasizes the "church" as an assembly of the "holy ones" called to live in communion with one another and to support one another (1 Cor 12:1–31; Rom 12:9–21). Individuals within the community will possess individual gifts, but the same Spirit is their source. These gifts exist to build up the community, promote true fellowship, and reinforce the group's holiness.

(8) Paul remains always aware of human sinfulness and frailty despite the superabundance of God's grace at work in the world (Rom 5:15–21). This conviction is tied to his teaching on justification by faith. It also relates to the tension between the "already" and "not yet" that marks his eschatological outlook. That is why he asserts the fact of salvation in Jesus Christ and yet continually exhorts his congregations to live out that salvation concretely in their lives.

78. Why does Paul seem to be against "speaking in tongues"? Isn't that a gift of the Holy Spirit?

Paul is not really against speaking in tongues as such, but against this phenomenon being raised to such a level that it overshadows other gifts of the Holy Spirit that are more important. It can become a source of false pride. Glossolalia probably refers to unintelligible sounds and words spoken in an ecstatic state rather than to foreign languages. Paul discusses this issue at length in a section of First Corinthians (chap. 14), while addressing the larger question of the purpose of spiritual gifts (chap. 12—14). Let me outline the broader scope of the question in order to place glossolalia in its proper context.

Paul's concern is that the Corinthian community has splintered into groups. In addition to creating competition, the divisions in the community also tended to highlight disagreements about whose spiritual gift was more important. Paul draws attention to three main principles about such gifts. First, all of them are from the same Spirit and for the purpose of building up the community (1 Cor 12:4–11; 14:26; cf. Rom 12:3–5). Consequently, they are not to build up the prestige of individuals who have such gifts. Second, each gift of the Spirit is important. None of the authentic gifts of the Spirit, whether teaching, prophecy, healing, or speaking in tongues, is inconsequential (1 Cor 12:11; cf. Rom 12:6–8). All can help build up the life of the Christian community. Finally, there is a hierarchy to these gifts. Although all can be authentic, some spiritual gifts are more important than others (1 Cor 12:28–31).

The problem that arose, however, was that some in the community thought that charismatic gifts such as speaking in tongues were more important. This attitude may come from the idea that unexplainable spiritual phenomena indicate a greater closeness to God and are therefore more significant to the community. Paul views all spiritual gifts differently. None of them compares to the importance of love, the greatest virtue that transcends all gifts, as expressed in the magnificent hymn to love (1 Cor 13). Love is the only way to exercise the gifts perfectly.

Where does speaking in tongues fit, then? Paul indicates that prophecy is a greater gift than speaking in tongues (1 Cor 14:2–5) because the purpose of prophecies is to instruct the community, while the primary purpose of speaking in tongues is to give honor and glory to God (1 Cor 14:2). Speaking in tongues most likely represents the groanings of the Holy Spirit made manifest in human voice. Consequently, I think Paul is placing the phenomenon of glossolalia in its proper context. He acknowledges it as something that should edify or build up the community rather than oneself (cf. 1 Cor 8:1; 10:23–24; 13:5). Speaking in tongues can manifest God's grandeur, but it does not take precedence over more important gifts. Paul goes so far as to say that, although he himself speaks in tongues far more than any of the Corinthians, he would rather speak five intelligible words than ten thousand unintelligible ones, if they help give instruction to the community (1 Cor 14:18–19).

79. Is Paul's description of what will happen at the end of time an accurate revelation of what will really take place?

I assume you have in mind a passage like one in First Thessalonians that seems to offer a detailed plan of what will happen in the final days when God's kingdom arrives in its fullness. It is worth quoting:

> For the Lord himself will descend from heaven with a cry of command, with the archangel's call, and with the sound of the trumpet of God. And the dead in Christ will rise first; then we who are alive, who are left, shall be caught up together with them in the clouds to meet the Lord in the air; and so we shall always be with the Lord. (1 Thess 4:16–17 RSV)

We must acknowledge that Paul, as well as most of the early Christians, expected the Lord's imminent return and the permanent establishment of his kingdom. Jesus himself expected it, and when he spoke of his return for judgment his followers naturally expected it to occur in rather quick order (Matt 16:27–28; 24:30; Mark 14:62). This expectation is known as the *parousia,* from the Greek word for "coming." When it did not occur as rapidly as anticipated, it caused great concern. Various Christian communities struggled with what scholars now call the "delay of the parousia."

Paul's treatment of this subject is interesting. On the one hand, he was influenced by this expectation. This apocalyptic mindset (see question 18) frames much of his ethical teaching (see Part Six). On the other hand, Paul also was concerned that his communities could become obsessed with the details of this expectation, and he has to warn them not to get preoccupied with these issues (1 Thess 5:1–2).

The response to your question needs to be placed in this context. Paul was very much a man of his own times. The imagery that he uses in First Thessalonians to describe the events of the end times is stock apocalyptic imagery from the OT (e.g., Joel 2:1–2; Zeph 1:15–16; Zech 9:14; Isa 27:13). These include such notions as a great shout, a trumpet blast, and the voice of an archangel. Some Christians even today interpret the imagery and sequence of events in a literal fashion. A whole series of popular fundamentalist books has explored this scenario in terms of being "left behind" (see the cover article in *Time* [July 1, 2002]). More likely, however, Paul is not offering a blueprint for the events of the kingdom but a standard apocalyptic vision of God's ultimate victory over evil at the end of time and the definitive establishment of the kingdom.

Even the image of meeting the Lord in the air makes sense in the three-layered universe of Paul's day where heaven was conceived as "up" and Sheol (the underworld) as "down." Of course, no one knows exactly how these events will take place, and Paul is no exception. While he acknowledges having had mystical experiences (e.g., 2 Cor 12:1–7), he prefers to put them in their proper perspective. His teaching on the "final days" fits into the traditional understanding of his time and does not need to be taken literally. The purpose of his words was to encourage hope in his communities that God's kingdom would indeed come (1 Thess 4:18, "console one another," NAB), but it would come "like a thief in the night" (1 Thess 5:2).

A final mention should be made of the word "rapture" that some communions use to describe this eschatological event. Given the incredible popularity of some modern literature among some Christians, like the *Left Behind* series of books, we need to address the contemporary notion of the rapture. The term comes from the Latin translation of 1 Thessalonians 4:17 (*rapere* = to seize, snatch) and it has become commonplace in fundamentalist circles. They have created a noun out of this verb to describe what they take to be the final events when Jesus comes the second (and final) time as judge of the world. The few who are saved—the Christian elect—will be snatched up to heaven, while the rest of humanity will go to eternal damnation. For good reason, scholars reject this elaborate scheme as far beyond the meaning of Paul's text. It makes a literal scenario out of what is really an indefinite apocalyptic vision of God's victory over evil. (For further information, see R. D. Witherup, "Wrestling with the Rapture," *Chicago Studies* 34:3 [1995] 251–61.)

80. But doesn't Paul teach that there will be a judgment day?

You are correct that Paul acknowledges belief in a day of judgment. His thought on this topic is not unique, however; it was consistent with much of the expectation of Judaism and the early church. Indeed, the concept of a "last judgment" remains an essential part of Christian faith today. It is intimately tied to Christian expectation of the parousia, the return of the Lord Jesus (2 Cor 5:10). Let's look at a few key concepts.

First, Judaism developed an expectation that there would be a judgment day. This is a natural part of the apocalyptic worldview that came into being in Judaism (question 18). Some of the OT prophets speak of "the day of the Lord," a day when God would arrive to set things right in the world and to punish evil (Isa 13:6; Joel 2:1; Amos 5:18–20). The primary purpose of this concept was to call people to accountability. The prophets tried to get people to be more obedient to God's will by threats of doom and judgment in the last days. Later developments of this thought evolved into a more elaborate scheme in which the day of judgment would bring reward for the righteous and condemnation to evildoers (Dan 12:2; Wis 3:1–4). The Gospels also exhibit characteristics of this thought in the teachings of Jesus (Matt 25:31–46; Mark 13:24–27). Most scholars acknowledge that Jesus himself was influenced by apocalyptic thought, as was Paul. Expectation of a final judgment was part and parcel of such a schema, and the teachings of Jesus and of Paul reflect this reality.

Paul expected "the day of the Lord"—the day of judgment—to come rather soon (1 Thess 5:2; 1 Cor 5:5; Phil 1:6). Paul sees this judgment day as promising two actions. Those who persist in doing evil will face terrible consequences, while those who are righteous will be rewarded and ultimately saved (Rom 2:7–8). Paul judges this to be God's righteous action vis-à-vis human beings who are to be held accountable for their thoughts, words, and especially their deeds. For Paul, both God (Rom 14:10) and Jesus Christ (2 Cor 5:10) will be involved in this judgment, for they both will occupy the "judgment seat" from whence judgment will be rendered on all who will be called forth for an accounting of their actions. Paul's favorite expression for the tone of this judgment day is a stern one. He speaks of the "wrath of God" (Greek *orgē;* Rom 1:18; 3:5). To be blunt, wrath is God's justified response toward human beings because of their persistent sinfulness (Rom 2:5; 13:4). It is a sign that God takes human actions seriously, and human behavior has consequences in the hereafter.

Paul also admits another kind of wrath or anger, namely, what human beings sometimes feel toward one another in certain circumstances. But contrary to God's justified wrath, Paul conceives of human wrath (Greek *thymos*) as a negative impulse that is to be avoided (Gal 5:20; Col 3:8). God, on the other hand, can be expected to execute judgment in a just fashion precisely because people bring this judgment on themselves (Rom 3:5). Paul also asserts that enemies who have worked against his proclamation of the gospel have brought God's wrath on themselves, much as those who persecuted the prophets and even Jesus himself (1 Thess 2:15–16). Yet wrathful judgment is not Paul's final word on the matter, stern as it is.

Paul also believes that Jesus desires to save all people and that his gracious action can save us from the wrath of judgment day. He proclaims that Jesus "rescues us from the wrath that is coming" (1 Thess 1:10; cf. Rom 5:9) with the assurance that "God has destined us not for wrath but for obtaining salvation through our Lord Jesus Christ" (1 Thess 5:9). The day of judgment holds forth both promise and doom. For those who live out the obedience of righteousness according to the law of love, salvation awaits them on the day of judgment. But eternal destruction will come upon those who refuse to change their evil ways. Paul acknowledges that God's judgments will ultimately be mysterious (Rom 11:33), but that all will have deserved their fate because God is just.

Note that Paul's teaching regarding judgment is mostly directed toward the indefinite future. Note also that he universally applies the threat of judgment to all, to Jew and Gentile alike (Rom 1–3). Paul firmly believed in the age to come, a basic tenet of Christian hope, but he also uses the theme of judgment as a warning or corrective to human ethical behavior ("disciplined," NRSV; 1 Cor 11:32; cf. 1 Cor 10:11). In a sense, Paul offers his readers both the carrot and the stick with regard to the coming judgment. It is something to fear and respect, yet it should not preoccupy our minds so much that we lose the focus of living in this world. To some degree, we are already being judged by the actions we take in reference to understanding how God has saved us in Jesus Christ. But Paul remains confident that our final destiny is God's salvation of us, and its fullness will one day be revealed (Rom 6:22–23).

Six

Paul's Ethics

81. Isn't Paul a pessimist when he describes human beings and their behavior?

No, Paul was not a pessimist; I think of him as a Christian realist. The clearest expression of what Paul has in mind is found at the beginning of the Letter to the Romans. After the customary greeting and thanksgiving, Paul explains his view that all humanity is under the power of sin. He demonstrates that Greeks (Gentiles) are under the power of sin, by listing the many symbols of idolatry and immorality in their culture (Rom 1:18–32). He draws attention to their feeble attempt to rely on human wisdom, a prominent feature in the Greco-Roman culture of his day. The result instead is folly and idolatry (Rom 1:22–23).

Lest the Jews in the community be tempted to ridicule the Greeks for their folly, he goes on to explain that despite their knowledge of good and evil from the Torah, they too are in need of God's salvation (Rom 2:1–3:8). Throughout his argumentation, Paul emphasizes that *all* are under the power of sin (Rom 3:9), although the order of addressing this issue is first the Jews and then the Greeks (Rom 1:16). In the end, all need salvation.

> There will be anguish and distress for everyone who does evil, the Jew first and also the Greek, but glory and honor and peace for everyone who does good, the Jew first and also the Greek. For God shows no partiality. (Rom 2:9–11)

He reinforces his point rhetorically with a question and an OT quote:

> What then? Are we any better off? No, not at all; for we have already charged that all, both Jews and Greeks, are under the power of sin, as it is written: "There is no one who is righteous, not even one; there is no one who has understanding, there is no one who seeks God." (Rom 3:9–11)

159

The use of the double expression, Jew and Greek, does not limit sinfulness and salvation to these people. That was simply the standard way of dividing the peoples of the world and therefore included all human beings.

Elsewhere in Romans Paul makes it clear that the human condition is one of sinfulness stemming from Adam's disobedience narrated in Genesis.

> Therefore just as one man's trespass led to condemnation for all, so one man's act of righteousness leads to justification and life for all. For just as by the one man's disobedience the many were made sinners, so by the one man's obedience the many will be made righteous. (Rom 5:18–19)

This is not a pessimistic view of the world but a theological view of what is wrong with humanity and what can cure it. Paul strongly believes that the one act of Jesus Christ—the new Adam—dying on the cross makes up for the one act of Adam, who sinned and brought all humanity with him into the tendency toward sinfulness. This position actually leads to Christian optimism. Paul continually sounds a note of "hope" that all will heed the message of the gospel, avoid sin, and attach themselves to the new life available in Jesus Christ. He does not think that God forces this attitude on humans. They retain the full freedom to accept or reject God's offer of salvation. Paul nonetheless believes that all are in need of it.

82. What does Paul mean by freedom?

Paul's understanding of freedom is quite different from our contemporary understanding. Modern American society tends to view freedom, in a broad fashion, as the ability to do whatever we want, when we want, and how we want. It is utter self-determination. No restrictions, no restraints, just the freedom to choose as we will and to live as we wish. Such a notion existed in Greco-Roman society in Paul's day, but Paul did not view freedom in this manner.

For Paul, freedom was not only "from" something (i.e., constraints) but also freedom "for" something (i.e., Jesus Christ). Paul contrasts freedom with slavery. Prior to the coming of Jesus, Paul says that the Jews were slaves to the law. He also acknowledges that Gentiles—who did not possess the law—at times fulfill the law because it is "written in their hearts" (Rom 1:15; cf. vv. 12–16). In Christ all are now free from the law, but with the responsibility to live in love. The Letter to the Galatians describes Paul's concept in some detail (chap. 5), of which two excerpts will illustrate the point.

> For freedom Christ has set us free. Stand firm, therefore, and do not submit again to a yoke of slavery. (Gal 5:1)

> For you were called to freedom, brothers and sisters; only do not use your freedom as an opportunity for self-indulgence, but through love become slaves to one another. For the whole law is summed up in a single commandment, "You shall love your neighbor as yourself." (Gal 5:13–14)

Remember the context of Galatians. Paul feared that his community was reverting to former practices, especially circumcision, under the influence of outsiders. He writes to clarify to the Galatians what true freedom in Christ now means. They are freed from the constraints of the law, but their new freedom entails the responsibility of living in love. Indeed, only love fulfills the demands of the law perfectly (Gal 5:14). In the midst of his argument, he makes a play on the notion of "slavery." Adherence to the Torah is literally a slavery to an antiquated understanding of God's will. Attaching oneself to Jesus Christ constitutes a new kind of "slavery"— living life according to the demands of obedience to love. Through baptism we become "slaves of Christ." I would diagram this two-sided understanding of freedom like this:

> *FROM* → TORAH, CIRCUMCISION =
> SLAVERY (to sin)
>
> FREEDOM→
>
> *FOR* → JESUS CHRIST, LIFE OF LOVE =
> "SLAVERY" (to Christ)

You can see, then, that Paul does not intend to give people a license to do whatever they want. Christian freedom has inherent responsibilities.

83. Why does Paul use the idea of becoming "slaves of Christ"? Doesn't that infringe on our personal freedom?

Not in Paul's thought. I should point out that the Greek word that Paul uses for slave *(doulos)* also means servant. Some translations interchange the words. Paul proudly calls himself a "slave of Jesus Christ" (Rom 1:1 NAB; NRSV "servant"; cf. Phil 1:1; 1 Cor 7:22), and the term applies to his colleagues as well (Col 1:7; 4:7, 12). Paul considers slavery to Christ to be a most freeing experience because one does not need to worry about fulfilling prescriptions of the law. Slavery to Christ means single-minded devotion to the will of God revealed in Jesus. This devotion also entails becoming "slaves" or servants to others (1 Cor 9:19; 2 Cor 4:5). It involves a choice between reverting to a real servitude to old ways, or a new and freeing "servitude" to the new ways revealed in Jesus.

> Do you not know that if you present yourselves to anyone as obedient slaves, you are slaves of the one whom you obey, either of sin, which leads to death, or of obedience, which leads to righteousness? But thanks be to God that you, having once been slaves of sin, have become obedient from the heart to the form of teaching to which you were entrusted, and that you, having been set free from sin, have become slaves of righteousness. (Rom 6:16–18)

Slavery in this sense is not a restriction of personal freedom but a free-choice commitment to Jesus Christ and all that he demands.

Attaching ourselves to Jesus Christ as his slaves or servants paradoxically frees us to be of broader service to those around us (cf. Jesus' own teaching in Matt 20:26–28).

84. What does Paul mean by the terms "spirit" and "flesh"?

Your question touches upon a broad area that is sometimes misunderstood. Let's look at each word individually before examining what they mean when used together.

When we hear the term "flesh," we likely think of something about sex. For us, the expression "sins of the flesh" connotes improper sexual activity. Paul, on the other hand, had a much broader understanding of this term. Paul can use the term "flesh" to refer to physical, corporeal existence, whether in reference to animals or to humans (1 Cor 15:39). In this sense it probably translates a Hebrew word *(basar),* which also means "flesh," but in relation to the body. Hebrew had no word for "body" other than flesh. The expression "flesh and blood" simply means physical human existence (1 Cor 15:50).

Beyond this physical meaning, Paul more often uses the term "flesh" to represent all that is corruptible, fleeting, and finite in this world. Flesh stands for the true weakness of human existence, especially when contrasted with divine existence. It is not, in this sense, restricted to the area of human sexuality. Although Paul would count sexual activity as one of the areas of "fleshly" preoccupations, he would not limit his observations to the sexual arena. All human existence is fleshly because it is finite; it does not last, it will come to an end.

"Spirit" also has a rather broad range of meanings. In the Greek *(pneuma)* as well as in its Hebrew counterpart *(ruach)* the word means "breath" or "wind"; thus something intangible yet able to be felt. When used of human beings, it means the inner core of one's being. It can mean the inner person, synonymous with the heart and soul of a person. In contrast, of course, it can also refer to the Holy Spirit (Rom 5:5; 15:13), or the Spirit of God

(Rom 8:14; 1 Cor 12:3). In Paul's thought, the divine spirit is different from the human spirit, but God's Spirit comes to dwell in the human person (1 Cor 6:19).

Sometimes spirit is synonymous with "soul" representing the inner identity of a human being, but we should remember that Paul did not make the standard distinction between body and soul that Greek philosophy made and that later Christian theology adopted. Paul retains a strongly Jewish understanding of the human person. Humans are animated bodies. They are not divided into body and soul; the two are united as one. Paul also uses the word "spirit" in a metaphorical sense when speaking of the "spirit of holiness" (Rom 1:4), the "spirit of slavery" (Rom 8:15), or the "spirit of gentleness" (1 Cor 4:21).

Most frequently, though, Paul uses spirit in contrast with flesh. The two words naturally belong together in Paul's thought. Here is where the contrast between spirit and flesh most clearly appears. Flesh represents being bound to sin, adhering to the law, and holding on to finite realities that will pass away. Spirit, on the other hand, means living according to God's will, living out Jesus' command to love one another, living according to the Holy Spirit, and setting one's heart on the kingdom that is to come. Romans and Galatians most frequently address this contrast. Two excerpts will illustrate.

> For those who live according to the flesh set their minds on the things of the flesh, but those who live according to the Spirit set their minds on the things of the Spirit. To set the mind on the flesh is death, but to set the mind on the Spirit is life and peace. For this reason, the mind that is set on the flesh is hostile to God; it does not submit to God's law—indeed it cannot, and those who are in the flesh cannot please God. But you are not in the flesh; you are in the Spirit, since the Spirit of God dwells in you. (Rom 8:5–9)

> Live by the Spirit, I say, and do not gratify the desires of the flesh. For what the flesh desires is opposed to the Spirit, and

what the Spirit desires is opposed to the flesh; for these are opposed to each other, to prevent you from doing what you want. But if you are led by the Spirit, you are not subject to the law. Now the works of the flesh are obvious: fornication, impurity, licentiousness, idolatry, sorcery, enmities, strife, jealousy, anger, quarrels, dissensions, factions, envy, drunkenness, carousing, and things like these. I am warning you, as I warned you before: those who do such things will not inherit the kingdom of God. By contrast, the fruit of the Spirit is love, joy, peace, patience, kindness, generosity, faithfulness, gentleness, and self-control. (Gal 5:16–23)

Romans 8, the great chapter on the Holy Spirit, urges the Christian to "walk not according to the flesh but according to the Spirit" (Rom 8:4; note the use of "walk" as a metaphor for "live"; cf. Gal 5:16). In First Corinthians Paul warns that holding on to attitudes that adhere to the flesh produces actions that harm the community: "…for you are still of the flesh. For as long as there is jealousy and quarreling among you, are you not of the flesh, and behaving according to human inclinations?" (1 Cor 3:3–4).

We can see from these examples that Paul finds the contrast between flesh and spirit to be central to his message. The focus is not on sexuality alone but on human behavior of all kinds. Spirit and flesh represent two opposite ways of living. We are called to live according to the Holy Spirit rather than according to the flesh (Rom 8:5).

85. I thought that Paul was very negative about sex. Isn't he preoccupied with sexual sins?

That is a common misunderstanding about Paul. I don't think he was preoccupied with sexual sins, but he had some strong concerns about sexual promiscuity or improper sexual behavior. First, though, I want to mention what Paul faced in the context of his Greco-Roman world.

Paul was an urban creature. He was born in a sizable city, and much of his ministry took place in urban environments. Many of the Greco-Roman cities Paul visited contained the usual opportunities for sexual promiscuity of all sorts, in the public and private arenas. Prostitution was particularly rampant in seaport towns, but it was also associated with certain pagan religious rituals. This was not new. The OT demonstrates that cultic prostitution associated with idolatrous worship was a constant struggle throughout Israel's history (e.g., Deut 23:18; Num 25:18; Hos 4:12–13; 9:1). Both Greek and Roman religions contained elements of sexual rituals associated with the pagan view that cultic prostitution would bring fertility to individuals and to the land. A city like Corinth, with the luxury of having two seaports, obviously had its reputation for wild living. The ancient Greek city of Corinth was particularly notorious for licentiousness, but it had been destroyed by the Romans in 146 B.C. The city Paul knew was the Roman city rebuilt by Julius Caesar in 44 B.C. Paul encountered numerous moral issues about sexuality there, but this would have been true of other cities he visited as well.

My point is that the secular environment in Paul's day was rather sexually promiscuous. (Has anything really changed?) If he comes across as being concerned about sexual behavior among his congregations, it is partly because his society faced such issues. In fact, different Greek philosophical schools in his day bemoaned the declining sexual mores of the culture. Christians faced many temptations in the area of human sexuality; some of them standard human temptations, and others with religious implications. Paul tries his best pastorally to address such situations with frankness.

To return to your question, I believe Paul's basic attitude toward human sexuality was a positive one. If we think he is *preoccupied* with this question, it is only because this was a question his congregations brought to him. Paul accepted the OT view that God had created males and females, and that the propagation of the human race by sexual intercourse was good and proper. He respects the body as the "temple of the Holy Spirit" (1 Cor 6:19) and urges his congregations to control their passionate desires in "holiness and honor" (1 Thess 4:4). But when sexual questions arose, Paul was not afraid to address them forthrightly.

For instance, at Corinth at least three issues emerged concerning human sexuality. One was a case of incest. Paul is so astounded at this case of incest that he indicates the only way to remedy it is to expel the perpetrator from the assembly (1 Cor 5:1–5). Even the pagans, he says, don't get so carried away (5:1). Another tendency in Corinth was the libertine attitude of some toward sexuality in general. They viewed it merely as a human appetite to be quenched. Paul quotes their policy and then refutes it because the human body is consecrated to God.

> "All things are lawful for me," but not all things are beneficial. "All things are lawful for me," but I will not be dominated by anything. "Food is meant for the stomach and the stomach for food," and God will destroy both one and the other. The body is meant not for fornication but for the Lord, and the Lord for the body. (1 Cor 6:12–13)

Paul lists some examples of this promiscuous attitude in Corinth, especially fornication, adultery, and homosexual prostitution (1 Cor 6:9). Notice, however, that he does so in the midst of drawing attention to other sins that are just as detrimental to people's spiritual health (as elsewhere, such as Rom 1:24–30). All sin is harmful to human beings, and sexual sins are part of the complex web of sin that infects humanity.

Paul mentions yet another attitude the Corinthians themselves brought to his attention that he also rejects. An opposite tendency to promiscuity also existed, namely, overly zealous ascetics (people who reject the attractions of the physical world and lead strict lives) who had the tendency to think that sexuality was bad. At the beginning of his lengthy address to this Corinthian problem as it related to marriage, Paul writes:

> Now concerning the matters about which you wrote: "It is
> well for a man not to touch a woman." But because of cases
> of sexual immorality, each man should have his own wife
> and each woman her own husband. The husband should
> give to his wife her conjugal rights, and likewise the wife to
> her husband....Do not deprive one another except perhaps
> by agreement for a set time, to devote yourselves to prayer,
> and then come together again, so that Satan may not tempt
> you because of your lack of self-control. (1 Cor 7:1–3, 5)

Not only does Paul approve of the mutual sexual relations within
marriage, but also his reasoning is interesting. Apparently he thinks
that the lack of a healthy sex life in a marriage could lead to seeking
gratification immorally elsewhere. He explicitly says to the unmarried, "But if they are not practicing self-control, they should marry.
For it is better to marry than to be aflame with passion" (1 Cor 7:9).
Does this sound like someone who is a prude? In my opinion, Paul
avoids both extremes with regard to human sexual behavior. He
rejects both sexual promiscuity and sexual prudery. But he remains
realistically aware of how potent a force human sexuality is and
how destructive it can be of the moral fiber of a society.

86. Didn't Paul also condemn homosexuality?

Your question is one of the most pastorally sensitive ones I
have had to tackle. The few passages where Paul speaks to this
issue deserve special scrutiny. Despite some scholarly attempts to
mitigate Paul's teaching on this moral question, I have to conclude that Paul opposed homosexual activity as morally wrong.
He saw it as a characteristic of the Gentile world that was abhor-
rent to Jews, and thus also unacceptable to followers of Jesus.
That being said, there are some nuances to this question that place
Paul's teaching in proper perspective.

First, I want to make two general observations. One must
notice how seldom the Bible itself speaks clearly of homosexuality. Only a handful of biblical texts mention it at all. In the OT

only two laws in Leviticus, in the context of the "Holiness Code," prohibit male homosexual activities (Lev 18:22; 20:13). These prohibitions occur in the midst of a series of other types of deeds that Israel deemed violations of God's covenant, such as dietary restrictions, lying, cheating, incest, cutting one's hair, and so on. Importantly, the Gospels do not portray Jesus speaking to the issue of homosexuality at all. In the absence of such mention, neither approval nor disapproval can be concluded. I think we can assume, however, that Jesus probably would have abided by the teaching in Leviticus. In the biblical world homosexuality was not a "hot topic" like it is today.

Second, people in the biblical world, including Paul, seem unaware of a distinction that we now make between explicitly homosexual activity and homosexual orientation. Nowhere does the Bible condemn homosexual orientation.

Third, no investigation of this delicate question can exclude discussion of some difficult vocabulary issues in the Greek text of the NT. Some technical distinctions and definitions cannot be overlooked. At times it is challenging to discover the exact meaning of the Greek expressions that Paul used. With these three cautions in mind, let's turn to Paul directly.

Paul speaks of this issue in only three specific texts: 1 Corinthians 6:9, 1 Timothy 1:10 [if genuine], and Romans 1:26–27. The first text lists two words that describe some form of homosexual activity. They are found in a list of deeds that Paul judges to be wrongdoing that now can be avoided because of the sanctification that Jesus Christ has achieved.

> Do you not know that wrongdoers will not inherit the kingdom of God? Do not be deceived! Fornicators, idolaters, adulterers, male prostitutes *(malakoi),* sodomites *(arsenokoitai),* thieves, the greedy, drunkards, revilers, robbers—none of these will inherit the kingdom of God. And this is what some of you used to be. But you were washed, you were sanctified, you were justified in the name of the Lord Jesus Christ and in the Spirit of our God. (1 Cor 6:9–11)

The two italicized Greek words are troublesome for translators. The first word, *malakoi,* literally means "soft ones," referring to effeminacy. It is not restricted to men who have feminine characteristics but is often used with reference to all things feminine that were considered less dignified than things masculine. In this context it may refer to males who offer themselves to other men for sexual penetration. Thus the translation "male prostitutes" is probably accurate.

The translation of *arsenokoitai* is another matter. The NRSV choice of "sodomites" is unfortunate. It wrongly invokes the image of the sin of Sodom and Gomorrah (Gen 19), which is not primarily about homosexuality but about general depravity and God's judgment. (Note, by the way, when Jesus uses the image of Sodom and Gomorrah the attention is only on God's judgment of these cities, not on the nature of the sin [Matt 11:23–24].) This Greek word combines two other words that literally mean "men-bedders." It is not clear that this literally refers to homosexual relations. More often the word occurs in contexts involving economic exploitation. Consequently, it *may* refer to sexual relations for economic gain, including male homosexual prostitution. It is not, however, an outright condemnation of homosexuality.

So what does the passage say? It lists five sexual and five other "wrongdoings." These are clearly actions to be avoided. But Paul goes on to say that some of the Corinthians used to be involved in such behavior (1 Cor 6:11), but now they have been justified and sanctified by Jesus Christ. His emphasis is on the positive change in their lives through their faith. Paul certainly frowns on all kinds of sexual sinfulness and other common sins, but he hardly singles out homosexuality for condemnation.

The second passage has a similar context. It lists a series of sins "contrary to sound teaching." Regardless of whether it genuinely stems from Paul himself or from a later hand, it falls within the Pauline tradition.

> This means understanding that the law is laid down not for the innocent but for the lawless and disobedient, for the godless and sinful, for the unholy and profane, for those who kill their father or mother, for murderers, fornicators, sodomites *(arsenokoitai),* slave traders, liars, perjurers, and whatever else is contrary to the sound teaching…. (1 Tim 1:9–10)

This list contains again the reference to *arsenokoitai* in the midst of a series of other sins. All of these are illustrations of disobedience and lawlessness. Nothing in the context necessarily requires a reference to homosexual relations, but it likely designates the same sin referred to in the aforementioned First Corinthians passage; namely, homosexual sex for money.

The final passage is the most serious. Paul writes to the Romans not only about male homosexual relations, but also about female homosexual relations. It is the only passage in scripture that mentions lesbianism. In the context of rehearsing how much evil exists in humankind, Paul writes about the consequences of human wickedness:

> For this reason God gave them up to degrading passions. Their women exchanged natural intercourse for unnatural, and in the same way also the men, giving up natural intercourse with women, were consumed with passion for one another. Men committed shameless acts with men and received in their own persons the due penalty for their error. (Rom 1:26–27)

This passage is very different from the previous two. This is no catalogue of sins but part of an explanation of the universal depravity of humankind and why people need faith. The catalogue of sins, however, is not far behind (vv. 29–31). When Paul speaks of "natural" and "unnatural" he is thinking of the created order of the universe as God intended it. He is not connoting a special revulsion at homosexual actions but a dramatic and sinful shift people have effected in the universe and that has shown itself in improper sexual behavior.

It is important to note why Paul mentions homosexual relations at all. Paul explains why the Gentiles are in need of God's righteousness.

> Therefore God gave them up in the lusts of their hearts to impurity, to the degrading of their bodies among themselves, because they exchanged the truth about God for a lie and worshiped and served the creature rather than the Creator.... (Rom 1:24–25)

Paul's concern is not primarily with homosexual behavior, but with idolatry. The Gentiles have turned the proper understanding of human life upside down. They no longer worship God as Creator but have substituted themselves and their desires in God's place. Homosexual activity is one among many symptoms of a society gone haywire. The "due penalty" (Rom 1:27) is thus not some disease that they bear in their bodies (the word is not used here) but the condition of being an idolater. Nor does Paul hold back strong words for the Jews in the Roman community, for he will equally challenge the Jews in Romans 2 about their lifestyles.

Paul, then, does not approve of homosexual activity. People who want to sweep away a negative view of homosexual *behavior* in the Bible are naive or misinterpret the textual evidence. Yet neither did Paul single out homosexual behavior for special condemnation. He assumed the traditional stance of the Jews toward homosexual behavior. In the Greco-Roman world homosexuality did not invoke the intense emotional reaction that it sometimes causes in contemporary Western societies. Paul, along with his contemporaries, conceived of homosexual activity as strictly a product of one's will. Sexual orientation was not the issue; the behavior was. For Paul, such behavior meant that people were under the power of sin, and that brought God's judgment upon them. Homosexual activity was one of several examples of the misorientation of his secular society.

There is a pastoral side to this question as well. Homosexuality is a volatile issue in our day. Many Christians inadvertently misuse the Bible when they say the Bible condemns homosexuals. Homosexuals deserve to be treated with human dignity as much as other human beings. We cannot invoke Paul for any kind of "gay bashing." In the context of the passage from Romans we have just examined, he also warns:

> Therefore you have no excuse, whoever you are, when you judge others; for in passing judgment on another you condemn yourself, because you, the judge, are doing the very same things. (Rom 2:1)

We too often forget that the other part of Paul's message was one of God's forgiveness. Paul speaks to the Romans about the misdirection of both the Greek and Jewish worlds so that he can announce to them the salvation of *all* (Rom 11:32).

87. Can you say more about Paul's view of marriage? Doesn't he say somewhere that divorce is OK sometimes?

Yes, Paul speaks of both marriage and divorce in a number of passages but none so thoroughly as 1 Corinthians 7. Obviously the question was of some concern to the Corinthians. I want to point out at the outset that Paul does not systematically address marriage and divorce. His discussion of these matters appears in the context of a larger discussion of human sexuality. Since he is dictating letters to address specific issues, we cannot expect the consistency or thoroughness of a treatise on the topic.

Paul clearly supported the traditional Jewish belief in monogamy. Men and women were created for one another for monogamous marriage until death separated them (Rom 7:2). Adultery was to be avoided, but the death of a spouse made a person free to remarry (Rom 7:3; 1 Cor 7:39). At the beginning of his response to the Corinthians' questions, Paul points out that he is aware of an instruction from the Lord (Jesus) about marriage and divorce:

> To the married I give this command—not I but the Lord—
> that the wife should not separate from her husband (but if
> she does separate, let her remain unmarried or else be recon-
> ciled to her husband), and that the husband should not
> divorce his wife. (1 Cor 7:10–11)

Paul acknowledges what modern scholars have concluded, that
Jesus himself took a strict view of marriage and prohibited
divorce (Matt 5:31–32; Mark 10:11–12; Luke 16:18). This attitude contrasted both with the practice of Judaism (which allowed
men to divorce their wives for serious reasons), and with the
Greco-Roman world (which allowed either spouse to divorce,
often for frivolous reasons). Although this passage uses two separate words to describe the action (separate, divorce), the meaning
appears to be the same, though some scholars would not agree.
Most interesting is that Paul allows for the possibility of a woman
separating from her husband. This practice was not Jewish but
Roman. In this regard Paul takes a more liberal attitude than we
might expect from his Jewish background.

　　Another aspect of Paul's teaching is the mutuality of marriage. Paul promoted the goodness of sexual relations within marriage. Sexual intercourse should not be withheld as a weapon in
some disagreement, although abstinence might be appropriate for
special reasons of prayer, and when agreed to mutually (1 Cor
7:5–6). Paul also urges reconciliation whenever possible. Then he
goes on to address the issue of the marriage between a pagan and
a Christian, in which he specifies his own regulation as compared
to the teaching of Jesus.

> To the rest I say—I and not the Lord—that if any believer
> has a wife who is an unbeliever, and she consents to live
> with him, he should not divorce her. And if any woman has a
> husband who is an unbeliever, and he consents to live with
> her, she should not divorce him. For the unbelieving hus-
> band is made holy through his wife, and the unbelieving
> wife is made holy through her husband. Otherwise, your

children would be unclean, but as it is, they are holy. But if
the unbelieving partner separates, let it be so; in such a case
the brother or sister is not bound. It is to peace that God has
called you. Wife, for all you know, you might save your husband. Husband, for all you know, you might save your wife.
(1 Cor 7:12–16)

This is the passage that Catholics refer to as "the Pauline privilege." It finds its way into the Catholic Church's canon law. In the
Church's eyes, however, it is not a divorce. It is a declaration of
nullity, that is, the marriage never really existed. Paul himself,
then, makes an exception to the absolute prohibition of divorce
that Jesus taught. Since God primarily desires that marriages be
peaceful, a separation is allowable in cases where the irreconcilable difference of religion interferes with the marriage.

Yet I emphasize that Paul still urges mutuality in the marriage so that both parties will work to save it. Verse 16 importantly challenges each party to consider that they might have a
positive effect on their partner with their religious convictions.
Paul does not promote this separation quickly, nor does he justify
it as really proper as a fulfillment of the ideal of marriage or of
Jesus' teaching. Paul is being pastorally expedient here in reluc-
tantly allowing this one exception to the rule. He does not consider divorce the ideal, but he recognizes that some circumstances
might require separation. In this sense, Paul permits a case of separation in response to the pastoral situation he encountered at
Corinth (cf. also Matt 19:9 for another exception). Nonetheless,
Paul strongly promoted the bond of monogamous marriage.

**88. Isn't Paul a chauvinist? Doesn't he think that women are
inferior to men? Isn't that why he sees the husband as the head of
the family and thus superior to the wife?**

Paul was a man of his day, and he lived in a society that basically considered women inferior to men. I believe to label Paul a
chauvinist, however, is simplistic and unfair. It passes a modern

judgment on an ancient figure who was bound to live in his culture and under its influences in ways that now strike some as antiquated. Furthermore, it does not do justice to Paul's teachings. For one thing, Paul has an awesome vision of the equality of *all* human beings by virtue of their belonging to Christ. He writes in Galatians:

> ...for in Christ Jesus you are all children of God through faith. As many of you as were baptized into Christ have clothed yourselves with Christ. There is no longer Jew or Greek, there is no longer slave or free, there is no longer male and female; for all of you are one in Christ Jesus. (Gal 3:26–28; see also Rom 10:12; Col 3:11)

This equality stems from Paul's theological view that baptism affects the very foundations of human existence. In Christ everything is made new. Life can no longer be lived in the same fashion as before: "So whoever is in Christ is a new creation: the old has passed away; behold, the new has arrived" (2 Cor 5:17 my translation; cf. Gal 6:15).

Paul is speaking of a dramatic theological vision of the way disciples of Jesus Christ operate within the church and society. Although this is not a direct attack on the social roles of his day, it is a challenge to view human interrelationships from a new vantage point. Distinctions according to race, social status, or gender are no longer the determining factors. Unity in Christ requires that we treat one another with human dignity and respect. Living out this vision, in fact, was extremely radical in Paul's day. It countered both Jewish and Gentile views of slaves and women as naturally inferior to free persons and to men. Even while Paul offers this Christian theological vision, at the same time he betrays some stereotypes common to his society. Paul lived in a world that viewed all authority in a hierarchical fashion, that is, shaped like a pyramid. At the top of the pyramid was God who is over all. Then came Christ, his Son and servant. In this hierarchical world, men held a higher position than women.

With regard to roles in marriage Paul exhibits some of the limitations of his world. He does in fact say: "But I want you to understand that Christ is the head of every man, and the husband is the head of his wife, and God is the head of Christ" (1 Cor 11:3). This is the only citation from the undisputed letters of Paul where Paul asserts that the husband is the head of the wife (not the family). Ephesians develops this theme in relation to marriage by directly comparing Christ as head of the church, with the husband being the head of the wife (Eph 5:23). This is primarily a passage on ecclesiology (i.e., the nature of the church) rather than on marriage. Marriage is used for purposes of analogy. If Ephesians is in fact Deutero-Pauline, then it reflects a later time when social roles of all kinds became more hierarchically ordered and structured. We should not blame Paul for what someone else may have written in his name. If Paul did, however, write this passage, then we need to consider it in the wider context of Paul's teaching about marriage. How should we understand these passages in their context?

The first passage from First Corinthians (11:3) is found in a lengthy section that deals with good order in liturgical gatherings. The specific issue in this section is wearing head coverings at prayer (see question 89). He is concerned to maintain traditions that have been handed down (1 Cor 11:2). The word "head" *can* connote the idea of authority over someone when it is used in a metaphorical sense. But here Paul is speaking about *origin*. Just as God is the origin of Christ, so is Christ the origin of man and man the origin of woman (see Gen 2:18–23). This is not a tract about the *subordination* of one to the other but of acknowledging their origin so that he can maintain distinctions between male and female roles in the church's order of worship. It is not a universal statement about the authority of the husband over his wife. Paul calls for a mutuality that must always be respected (1 Cor 11:11–12).

The next important passage is the famous Deutero-Pauline passage on marriage. Many women, especially, cringe when they hear the words,

> Wives, be subject to your husbands as you are to the Lord.
> For the husband is the head of the wife just as Christ is the
> head of the church, the body of which he is the Savior. Just
> as the church is subject to Christ, so also wives ought to be,
> in everything, to their husbands. (Eph 5:22–24)

But two problems reinforce a misinterpretation of this passage.
First, we hear it out of context. We ignore important lines found at
both ends of this passage that are meant to apply to *all* believers
and not just to married couples. The author first says in the previous verse, "Be subject to one another out of reverence for Christ"
(v. 21). Even more significant is the context of the whole of chapter five. The chapter begins with the overarching command,
"Therefore be imitators of God as beloved children, and live in
love, as Christ loved us and gave himself up for us..." (Eph
5:1–2). At the other end of the passage, we overlook the striking
command to husbands: "Husbands, love your wives, just as
Christ loved the church and gave himself up for her..." (Eph
5:25; see also vv. 28 and 33). Sandwiched between these two contexts our problematic passage takes on new light. Both parties in
the marriage are called mutually to the task of relating in a loving
manner. Both are bound to imitate God in the way of love, the
husband no less than the wife.

Second, our modern ears do not necessarily hear what the
original readers would have heard in the command "be subject to"
(used of both parties). The NAB translates the word "be subordi-
nate to" but this is not the only possible translation. The word has
less to do with power than it does with *respect* or *allegiance*. (The
final command to wives in the passage in fact is to "respect" their
husbands [v. 33].) The verb "be subject to" actually occurs three
times in this passage. It is applied to the mutual relationship
between husband and wife (v. 21), to the relationship of the wife
to the husband (vv. 22, 24), and to the relationship of the church to
Christ (v. 24). The threefold command of husbands to love their
wives provides an important counterbalance to the threefold command of wives to be subject to or respect their husbands. Since

Paul clearly considers love the highest and most demanding of virtues (1 Cor 13:13), I would say that Paul is not demanding less of husbands than of wives. But we must also admit that Paul lived in a society where marital roles were distinguished with care. Nevertheless, his teaching about mutuality in marriage, coupled with his radical view of the unity of all in Christ, should make us cautious about applying a modern label such as "chauvinist" to characterize him.

89. Why does he tell women that they have to wear hats in church or that they should not speak in church?

You are referring to two more passages in First Corinthians where Paul addresses specific issues in the church at Corinth. I confess that the exact situation Paul is addressing in each instance is obscured by the passage of time. Both passages occur in a lengthy section where Paul has grouped together concerns about order in worship at Corinth (1 Cor 11—14). Let's look at each passage separately.

The first passage contains an example of Paul's complex reasoning and rabbinic style of scriptural interpretation. Paul addresses the issue of head coverings (1 Cor 11:2–16). He does not limit himself to comments about women but also about men. Certain customs with regard to hairstyle were important in Paul's day, even though Paul says these are not universally respected in the "churches of God" (v. 16). He urges the Corinthians to judge for themselves (v. 13). Men should have short hair and not have their head covered. Women should have long hair and have their head covered. Paul interweaves his comments about both throughout the passage. Not only does he make reference to traditions that are to be maintained (v. 2), but he also gives a biblical rationale from the OT. Clearly having the creation of humankind narrated in Genesis 2:18–25 in mind, Paul says,

> For if a woman will not veil herself, then she should cut off her hair; but if it is disgraceful for a woman to have her hair

> cut off or to be shaved, she should wear a veil. For a man ought not to have his head veiled, since he is the image and reflection of God; but woman is the reflection of man. Indeed, man was not made from woman, but woman from man. Neither was man created for the sake of woman, but woman for the sake of man. For this reason a woman ought to have a symbol of authority on her head, because of the angels. (1 Cor 11:6–10)

Paul's view at first glance seems to exalt men above women again. But if that were the case, he would not go on in the next two verses to make a strong statement about the mutuality between men and women that God ordained at creation.

> Nevertheless, in the Lord woman is not independent of man or man independent of woman. For just as woman came from man, so man comes through woman; but all things come from God. (1 Cor 11:11–12)

I confess that Paul's mention of angels in his argument at this point is obscure. No one has been able to explain definitively how angels apply to the situation Paul addresses, but angels might represent some sort of "guardians of authority" who are present when the assembly meets and therefore are entrusted to watch over proper authoritative etiquette.

In any case, this passage is not about wearing hats in church. In fact, despite the translations, the word "veil" in Greek is not used; the expression used refers to covering and uncovering. In all likelihood, there was a cultural issue involved as well as an ecclesial one. The real concern is about honor and shame. Something is occurring during worship in Corinth that Paul feels brings shame upon the community. He strives to correct the situation with his instruction. In the Greco-Roman world women wore long hair and usually "veiled" it, not with a head covering necessarily, but by binding it up, perhaps at times in braids. Free-flowing long hair was considered shameful and flirtatious, and it may have been associated with pagan ecstatic practices. But excessively short hair was associated with lesbians and prostitutes. Apparently at Corinth some women were abandoning the practice of keeping their hair bound while praying or prophesying. In effect, Paul says that unbinding their hair in public at worship is shameful; they might as well shave their heads and make themselves disreputable women. He advises instead that they abide by the cultural norms of propriety. When we remember that one of Paul's primary concerns with the Corinth church was the tendency for division, his words here make more sense. Paul doesn't want changes in customs to become so disruptive in worship that people are distracted. He is not making a universal policy about what women should wear to church.

The second passage, at first, seems even more serious. Paul appears to prohibit women from public speaking in church. He says,

> (As in all the churches of the saints, women should be silent in the churches. For they are not permitted to speak, but should be subordinate, as the law also says. If there is anything they desire to know, let them ask their husbands at home. For it is shameful for a woman to speak in church....)
> (1 Cor 14:33–35)

The first thing to notice is the presence of parentheses. The NRSV translators (unlike the RSV and NAB) judge this statement to be an aside in the midst of Paul's larger concern; namely, maintaining orderly worship (v. 33). Some scholars think these lines are interjected into Paul's letter by an author from a later time. That may be the case, but I think it unlikely. The problem is that these words appear to contradict what Paul says elsewhere in the same letter. Paul presumes that women can and do speak at worship, both at prayer and at prophecy (1 Cor 11:5, 13). This would be a change in practice from the normal Jewish prohibition of women speaking in the synagogue. Given the large number of women in Paul's churches and among his own colleagues, it is unlikely that he means here they should have no public role in worship. It is possible, however, that Paul means to exclude women from certain formal conversations that dealt with administrative matters in the assembly. Again we do not know the exact situation Paul has in mind with these words. It is also possible that the verb "speak" (v. 35) refers not to public speaking but to normal conversation. If this is so, then Paul could be referring to gossip or disruptive conversation.

In sum, Paul is less restrictive of women than we make him out to be. Part of the problem is not fully understanding the customs of Paul's day, which, in any case, are not to be considered valid for all time. Another problem is that our modern ears hear some of these passages in ways that differ from the way Paul's original hearers would have received them. I prefer to give Paul the benefit of the doubt and to concentrate on his very positive images of the unity of all people in Christ, regardless of economic or social status or gender (Gal 3:28).

90. If Paul is as radical a visionary as you say, then why does he condone slavery?

Most of the time Paul uses the vocabulary of slavery in a metaphorical sense that we have previously mentioned (question 83; for example, see Rom 6:16–20). When he refers to slavery in a literal sense, I think we should be cautious about how we speak of Paul's attitude. I don't think he condoned slavery. He acknowledged it as a societal reality. The ramifications of his theological perspective, however, were actually subversive to his society's acceptance of human slavery.

One passage where Paul speaks of slavery is in the context of his urging everyone to stay just as they are because the world is quickly coming to a close (1 Cor 7:21–24). Slavery is a condition to be tolerated (also 2 Cor 11:20). Paradoxically, slaves who are Christian really become free inwardly while free persons who are Christian become "slaves" of Christ (1 Cor 7:22–23).

The later Deutero-Pauline writings also reinforce the mainte-
nance of the social structures, including slavery (Eph 6:5–8;
1 Tim 6:1; Titus 2:9). They command masters to treat their slaves
with fairness (Col 4:1; Eph 6:9). Everyone, both master and
slave, has the same eternal "master" in heaven (Eph 6:8–9). The
early Christians simply presumed that slavery was part of the
order of the universe. That mentality reigned supreme for nine-
teen centuries. We can hardly be critical only of Paul for support-
ing an institution that dehumanized large segments of
populations because they were deemed as chattel. But another
aspect of Paul's view is pertinent and much more radical. I will
point out three characteristics.

1. Paul takes the word "slave" and makes of it a metaphor
for utter commitment to Christ. He insists that being called to
freedom means, paradoxically, committing ourselves to a new
kind of slavery, the slavery of love.

> For you were called to freedom, brothers and sisters; only do
> not use your freedom as an opportunity for self-indulgence,
> but through love become slaves to one another. For the
> whole law is summed up in a single commandment, "You
> shall love your neighbor as yourself." (Gal 5:13–14)

Part of Paul's brilliance was the ability to take a common concept
and transform it into a majestic metaphor for the newness of the
Christian life. Paul thus transformed the language of slavery in
his own day.

2. Paul proudly quotes an older tradition that Jesus humbled
himself to become a slave (Phil 2:7) so that we could also humble
ourselves in servitude to righteousness. Paul was not ashamed to
adopt the language of slavery and servitude for the type of humble service that Christ offered humanity, and that his followers are
asked to imitate (Phil 2:5).

3. Paul's little Letter to Philemon packs one big punch with
regard to slavery. The issue Paul addresses in this, the most personal of his letters, seems to be that he is sending a runaway slave

(Onesimus) back to his master (Philemon). This was a dangerous move, for runaway slaves could be harshly treated if caught and returned. They could be beaten, killed, branded, flogged, or sold. Paul, however, urges Philemon to take Onesimus back "no longer as a slave but more than a slave, a beloved brother" (Phlm 16). This is actually a subversive gesture. Paul had converted Onesimus in prison and wanted to keep him as a colleague, but he decided to send him back. Paul uses every persuasive argument he can muster to convince Philemon to treat Onesimus differently, now that he is a Christian. Paul even resorts to some not-so-subtle arm-twisting:

> If he has wronged you in any way, or owes you anything, charge that to my account. I, Paul, am writing this with my own hand: I will repay it. I say nothing about your owing me even your own self. Yes, brother, let me have this benefit from you in the Lord! Refresh my heart in Christ. Confident of your obedience, I am writing to you, knowing that you will do even more than I say. One thing more—prepare a guest room for me, for I am hoping through your prayers to be restored to you. (Phlm 18–22)

Not only does Paul offer to repay any loss for the slave, but he also reminds Philemon that he himself is indebted to Paul in some way. Philemon owes Paul a favor, and Paul basically says, "I'll be paying you a visit." Is this Paul's way of saying he'll check up to make sure that Onesimus is properly treated?

My point is that on one level Paul upholds the institution of slavery in his day. On a deeper level, however, he understood that the implication of the gospel of Jesus Christ is that all are free. Of all the contrasts he included in the freedom of Christ, slaves and free persons receive as much mention as Jews and Greeks, males and females (1 Cor 12:13; Gal: 3:28; Col 3:11). If it took the Christian church centuries to put this lesson into practice, it was not Paul's fault.

91. Why does Paul talk about the Jewish food laws? Aren't they irrelevant to Christians?

Yes, Paul's teachings about Jewish dietary laws are not particularly relevant to our present situation any more than the laws of the Book of Leviticus are binding upon Christians. But Paul has other reasons to address the issue of the dietary laws. You will recall that Paul makes the point in Galatians that James, Kephas (the Aramaic name for Peter), and John had given Paul the green light to evangelize the Gentiles without requiring circumcision. Then Paul recounts how Peter withdrew from table fellowship with Gentiles under pressure from Jewish Christians (Gal 2:11–14). The text never explicitly mentions the Jewish dietary laws as the problem, but this was likely the reason for the embarrassing breach of etiquette. Paul apparently did not insist that his Gentile converts keep a kosher table. He ridicules in the strongest terms Peter's hypocrisy as giving in to pressure from the Jewish Christians on this matter.

Elsewhere the issue arises from a different perspective. In Corinth some Christians were having scruples about eating meat that previously had been sacrificed to idols (1 Cor 8). It was a common practice that some meat used in pagan ceremonies would later become available in the marketplace. Jewish regulations forbade consuming such food. Paul gives the Corinthians two important perspectives to be their guide. On the one hand, food itself is not important: "'Food will not bring us close to God.' We are no worse off if we do not eat, and no better off if we do" (1 Cor 8:8). On the other hand, Paul is concerned that if some of the more scrupulous members of the community are scandalized by the eating of idol meat, and thereby tempted to return to pagan worship, he hopes that the Corinthians will have the sense to refrain from the practice.

> But take care that this liberty of yours does not somehow become a stumbling block to the weak….Therefore, if food

> is a cause of their falling, I will never eat meat, so that I may
> not cause one of them to fall. (1 Cor 8:9, 13)

Of utmost concern is not bringing scandal to the "weaker" members of the community. Paul does not want to encourage more factional divisiveness among the Corinthians. The food regulations themselves are quite secondary. He says virtually the same thing in 1 Corinthians 10:23–33.

In his most theological letter, Romans, Paul reiterates the same message but adds an even clearer statement that the nature of the food in itself is not the question. Nevertheless some people have scruples that must be recognized.

> I know and am persuaded in the Lord Jesus that nothing is
> unclean in itself; but it is unclean for anyone who thinks it
> unclean....Do not, for the sake of food, destroy the work of
> God. Everything is indeed clean, but it is wrong for you to
> make others fall by what you eat; it is good not to eat meat
> or drink wine or do anything that makes your brother or sis-
> ter stumble. (Rom 14:14, 20–21)

The main issue for the Romans as well as for the communities Paul himself founded was one of promoting Christian unity: "Let us therefore no longer pass judgment on one another, but resolve instead never to put a stumbling block or hindrance in the way of another" (Rom 14:13).

Unfortunately, many Christians have never taken Paul's message to heart. It is so easy to place the incidentals of life first and forget the essentials. When Paul speaks of dietary regulations, it is not to keep them before the Christian community as an ideal. On the contrary, Paul was merely addressing a specific issue for some of his communities, and he did so with considerable nuance and flexibility.

92. How do Paul's moral teachings compare with those of Jesus? Didn't Paul have to follow what Jesus taught?

On the whole, Paul's moral teachings resemble those of Jesus quite closely. Some of the questions we have answered should show that Paul sometimes makes a distinction between what he got from the Lord and his own perspective. Keep in mind that we do not know how much of the "Jesus tradition" Paul knew. Yet his general moral principles are quite consistent with what Jesus taught. Primary among Paul's teachings is the command to love.

> Owe no one anything, except to love one another; for the one who loves another has fulfilled the law. The commandments, "You shall not commit adultery; You shall not murder; You shall not steal; You shall not covet"; and any other commandment, are summed up in this word, "Love your neighbor as yourself." Love does no wrong to a neighbor; therefore, love is the fulfilling of the law. (Rom 13:8–10)

These words echo closely Jesus' own call to put love above all other things (Matt 19:18–19; 22:39; Mark 12:31).

In the previous question we saw that in regard to food laws Paul urged his congregations to put essential matters first. That attitude resembles Jesus' own urging to place the essentials first (Mark 7:1–15). Paul's use of the notion of slave or servant that we have already discussed (question 83) also brings to mind Jesus' teaching that whoever would be the greatest must become the servant of all the rest (Matt 18:1–4; Mark 9:35; 20:26; Luke 22:26).

Paul certainly sees himself and his teachings in continuity with what Jesus taught. He feels confident that his gospel is consistent with the traditions he has inherited. Indeed, the risen Lord is the one who commissioned him for his proclamation of the gospel (Gal 1:11–12). Where he adapts the teachings of Jesus to the needs of his individual communities, he does so with full understanding of being faithful to the essence of the Christian message.

Some suggest that Paul's distortion appears in the very concept of the church. Jesus came and preached the gospel, but Paul preached the church instead. The implication seems to be that the church's teaching is not related to that of Jesus. Can we say that the church does not flow from the teachings of Jesus? Historical studies indicate that Jesus gathered twelve disciples around him to constitute a new community, modeled after the twelve tribes of Israel (Mark 3:14; Luke 6:13; cf. Matt 19:28–29; Luke 22:30). In addition, Jesus' teachings about the demands of discipleship also indicate that a new community springs forth, one in which even blood relationships are secondary to the relationship established by baptismal bonds (Mark 3:31–25; Matt 12:46–50). Paul clearly conceives of the church as the body of believers in Jesus Christ who are called to live out the demands of love (1 Cor 12—13). What he has done is taken Jesus' teachings and applied them to his communities for the sake of building up the body of Christ.

In conclusion, then, Paul's ethics, and his teaching in general, are quite consistent with the moral teaching of Jesus, even if they are adapted to meet the situations he encountered. I would not agree with those throughout history who have maligned Paul for distorting the message of Jesus.

93. Paul speaks of faith, hope, and love, but the greatest is love. Doesn't that really summarize his ethical teaching?

In some ways it does. The NT has no more profound reflection on the nature of love than Paul's "hymn" to it in 1 Corinthians 13. Little wonder that this passage is one of the most frequently used biblical passages at weddings. But we tend to romanticize it more than I think Paul would have.

Paul definitely singles out three virtues that are critical to the Christian life: faith, hope, and love (1 Cor 13:13). Generally this is the ordering of these three virtues. Love is last in the list because it is the most important. But in First Thessalonians Paul speaks of a different order: faith, love, and hope (1 Thess 1:3; 5:8). The reason for this is that a primary concern for the Thessalonians was the loss of hope in the face of the death of some members of the community. Paul writes to console them and to encourage their hope in the future (1 Thess 4:13—5:11). Generally, though, Paul retains the order of the three virtues that has become traditional. But what does Paul mean by them? Paul is not being romantic in placing love above the other virtues. All three are essential. Let's look at how he speaks of them at the beginning of First Thessalonians.

> We always give thanks to God for all of you and mention you in our prayers, constantly remembering before our God and Father your work of faith and labor of love and steadfastness of hope in our Lord Jesus Christ. (1 Thess 1:2–3)

Paul singles out three aspects of these virtues: *work* of faith, *labor* of love, and *steadfastness* of hope. The virtues are not easily maintained. One must work at them, be faithful to the task, and endure over time. In the same letter he uses the image of putting on armor to do battle with the forces of evil. In contrast to those in darkness, Christians live in the light. They arm themselves with the virtues so that they can be effective in their mission to the world. "But since we belong to the day, let us be sober, and put on the breastplate of faith and love, and for a helmet the hope of salvation" (1 Thess 5:8).

Faith is primarily for Paul a personal relationship with God and with Jesus Christ. It is free obedience to Christ and being configured to his life. Faith in Jesus Christ contrasts with reliance in the OT upon the law (Gal 2:16). It is not so much a noun, which is focusing on the content of faith, as it is a verb, a dynamic relationship with the risen Lord. It is an act of utter trust in God.

Hope is the attitude of expectant confidence that God will remain faithful to age-old promises. Hope does not arise from actually seeing the tangible reality that is hoped for. Rather, hope requires patient awaiting of the revelation of that which is unseen (Rom 8:24–25). It might be likened to the future tense of faith. It also entails a positive attitude that helps one endure life's trials and tribulations (Rom 5:4).

Love is that perfect conformity and obedience to God's will that respects others and freely embraces them. "Love does no wrong to a neighbor; therefore love is the fulfilling of the law" (Rom 13:10). Love builds up the community (1 Cor 8:1) and surpasses all other gifts or talents (1 Cor 13:1–3). It is the first fruit of the Holy Spirit (Gal 5:22). Paul is quite concrete about the demands of love. It causes no scandal (Rom 14:13–15) and requires direct action toward one another in the community (1 Thess 4:9). Love really does sum up all the virtues and puts them into action. It is the engine that drives the morality of the gospel of Jesus Christ. It constitutes the very moral fiber of our human existence.

94. Paul comes across as intolerant of sinners. Isn't he overly strict with them?

Paul has a lot to say about sin and sinners, but I would not say he was intolerant of them. He counts himself among those sinners who have struggled to do the right thing and found themselves nonetheless mired in sinful activity. In a famous first-person passage Paul describes what I take to be his own struggle and simultaneously that of humanity's universal grappling with sin.

> I do not understand my own actions. For I do not do what I want, but I do the very thing I hate. Now if I do what I do not want, I agree that the law is good. But in fact it is no longer I that do it, but sin that dwells within me. For I know that nothing good dwells within me, that is, in my flesh. I can will what is right, but I cannot do it. For I do not do the good I want, but the evil I do not want is what I do. Now if I do what I do not want, it is no longer I that do it, but sin that dwells within me. (Rom 7:15–20)

Paul understands well the paradox of knowing what is right but being unable to do it. Notice that he often uses the word "sin" in the singular, denoting a power beyond ourselves that can rule over us. He also uses the plural at times to designate individual sinful actions (Rom 3:25; 1 Cor 15:3), but he concentrates on sin as an external power that has dominated human activity from the time of the first sinner, Adam (Rom 5:12–14). The reason Paul concentrates so much effort on sin is that sin brought death into the world. Sin, death, and darkness all work against the gospel of Jesus Christ. But his view is not entirely negative. He also says that "where sin increased, grace abounded all the more" (Rom 5:20). More importantly, "But God proves his love for us in that while we still were sinners Christ died for us" (Rom 5:8). Paul does not think that we have to change our lives in order for God to act graciously toward us. Just the reverse: Even while we remained sinners, God acted graciously on our behalf in Christ. So Paul informs his readers they should consider themselves "dead to sin and alive to God in Christ Jesus" (Rom 6:11).

Yet Paul is ever the realist. He recognizes that sin appears in all forms of evil human thoughts, words, and actions. He can catalogue all the terrible deviances of his day with the thoroughness of an encyclopedist (Rom 1:25–31; 2:21–23). Both Jew and Gentile alike are under the power of sin (Rom 3:9), yet he knows that God's action of giving his own Son to the world has brought new life and the possibility of rejecting sin and living in the law of love. He contrasts the effects of sin with the effects of God's gift: "For the wages of sin is death, but the free gift of God is eternal life in Christ Jesus our Lord" (Rom 6:23). Who would not prefer life to death? Paul cannot conceive that the choice itself is easily misunderstood. He remains realistic, though, that all too often people choose sin over goodness.

One more aspect of his recognition of human frailty deserves mention. Pastorally, Paul knew that imparting the Christian faith to his communities took time and effort. He proceeded in stages. He speaks, for instance, of his first encounters with the Corinthians and how he demanded of them only what they could take at the time.

> And so, brothers and sisters, I could not speak to you as spiritual people, but rather as people of the flesh, as infants in

Christ. I fed you with milk, not solid food, for you were not
ready for solid food. Even now you are still not ready, for
you are still of the flesh. For as long as there is jealousy and
quarreling among you, are you not of the flesh, and behaving according to human inclinations? (1 Cor 3:1–3)

He uses one of his favorite contrasts between "spiritual" and
"fleshly" existence to indicate that the Corinthians had a tendency
to hold on to their sinful inclinations. These promoted factionalism in the community. Paul says that they were like infants who
need milk rather than solid food. As Paul proceeds in his letter he
makes it clear that they are to grow up, to become spiritually
mature adults. We might say that Paul uses the proverbial "carrot
and stick" in dealing with his communities. He demonstrates his
pastoral sensitivity to their situation, but then he calls them to
respond more appropriately to one another in a Christian fashion.
This is not a rigorous approach, intolerant of sinners. Neither is it
a laissez-faire mentality that allows people to sit back and rest on
their laurels.

**95. Can you say more about the kinds of sins Paul thought should
be avoided? Are some more important than others?**

As with any good instructor of morality, Paul recognized
that there were some sins that were obviously more destructive
than others. There is a hierarchy of sinfulness. But Paul does not
shy away from being very explicit with his communities.

First, we should notice that Paul has a general view of the
human condition that affects our view of sin. Human beings, he
says, are under the influence of this world and too often prefer
human wisdom to divine wisdom (1 Cor 1:18–31; 2:6–7), and this
leads them to do foolish actions that show their dependence upon
the "powers" of this world rather than the "power" of God (cf.
Rom 8:38; Eph 6:12; Col 1:6 with 1 Cor 1:18; Rom 1:16). When
people allow themselves to come under any power other than
God's, they are led to idolatry—an evil that shows itself in many

different forms. Paul likely detested idolatry because of his Jewish heritage. The first basic tenet of Israel is that there is only one God (Deut 5:6–7; 6:4) and anything that tries to displace God in the human arena is to be rejected as an idol. Specifically, Paul rejects any attraction to pagan idols such as those in pagan temples or attached to pagan rituals (1 Cor 8:1–13).

Paul had a much larger view of the power of sin (Rom 3:9) than simply idolatry. In various settings Paul lists the kinds of sinfulness common in his day that proved bothersome to his communities. At times, Paul addresses certain kinds of sinfulness because he has been asked to do so by certain communities or has heard of problems that he wishes to correct. This is especially the case in First Corinthians, where a large part of the letter is devoted to specific problems plaguing the Corinthians (1 Cor 5—11). But he also points out lists of vices that are to be avoided.

Romans contains two of the most comprehensive lists. After addressing briefly the question of homosexuality in the Greco-Roman world (see question 86), he lists the following vices that often accompany self-degradation among the Gentiles:

> And since they did not see fit to acknowledge God, God gave them up to a debased mind and to things that should not be done. They were filled with every kind of wickedness, evil, covetousness, malice. Full of envy, murder, strife, deceit, craftiness, they are gossips, slanderers, God-haters, insolent, haughty, boastful, inventors of evil, rebellious toward parents, foolish, faithless, heartless, ruthless. (Rom 1:28–31)

This is quite a list of faults. But notice that Paul admits at the very beginning that the perpetrators refused to "acknowledge" God properly. It reminds one of the sin of Adam. The creature loses sight of the Creator. This leads to all kinds of evil deeds.

He is no less stern with his fellow Jews. In the same letter he focuses on the age-old problem of people who do not put into practice what they teach. He warns them against the hypocrisy that shows itself when they forbid stealing, adultery, idolatry, and breaking the law, but engage in it themselves (Rom 2:17–23). All these evils, whether performed apart from the law (as with the Gentiles) or under it, bring ruin to the perpetrators.

Elsewhere Paul also lists other vices that are to be avoided because they are of the "flesh" rather than the "spirit." That is, they are rooted in this passing corrupt world rather than in the world to come.

> Now the works of the flesh are obvious: fornication, impurity, licentiousness, idolatry, sorcery, enmities, strife, jealousy, anger, quarrels, dissensions, factions, envy, drunkenness, carousing, and things like these. I am warning you, as I warned you before: those who do such things will not inherit the kingdom of God. (Gal 5:19–21; cf. Col 3:5)

Again, the list is a compendium of typical kinds of sinfulness that were prevalent in Paul's day. But we would also have to admit that the listing is not all that unfamiliar in our own time. The fact is that Paul's catalogue of sins can be considered quite ordinary. There aren't many "original" sinners left in the world. Paul's list of sins is as applicable today as ever. One should not forget, however, that Paul balances this latter list with a similar list of virtues that disciples of Jesus are expected to put into practice and that clearly counterbalance evil deeds (Gal 5:22).

Finally, I point out that the Deutero-Pauline letters pick up on this phenomenon from a slightly different angle. They contain what scholars call "household codes." These are more formal lists of ethical exhortations that are important for maintaining the stability of the church (and lawful society). Thus, specific ethical advice is given to husbands, wives, children, masters, and slaves (see especially Col 3:18—4:1; Eph 5:22–33; 1 Tim 2:1–15). Though these are more fully developed in the Deutero-Pauline letters, their inspiration may have come from Paul's undisputed letters, for he expresses his desire that ethical behavior build up and maintain the "household" of God (Gal 6:10; "family of faith," NRSV and NAB; cf. 1 Thess 5:11; 1 Cor 14:4). Paul's basic stance toward sinfulness is also at home in his cultural world. Some Greek philosophical schools taught that certain ethical practices were to be avoided, while others helped create a harmonious life. Paul is not above mentioning them at least in the background of his teaching (e.g., 1 Thess 4:9–12). Now is there a hierarchy to Paul's lists of sins? I don't think so. Yes, Paul recognizes that some sinful deeds are more serious than others, but more important is the general attitude: Put your faith in action by a righteous life, and you will attain the kingdom of God. We should not forget, too, that Paul has a practical side to his moralizing about sin. Sinning is not only bad for the self, but it wrongly influences others. One should avoid sin as much so as not to give scandal—especially to those who lack a strong moral fiber—as much as to protect one's own uprightness (1 Cor 8:9–13; Rom 14:13–16). And he certainly calls his congregations to avoid judging others too harshly, because all have sinned and are therefore worthy of being forgiven by God (Rom 2:1; 14:13).

96. What does Paul teach about reconciliation?

Paul has a profound understanding of reconciliation. He directly ties the reconciliation of God to the salvation that God has wrought in Christ (Rom 5:10–11). Second Corinthians contains the most extended reference to Paul's view.

So if anyone is in Christ, there is a new creation: everything old has passed away; see, everything has become new! All this is from God, who reconciled us to himself through Christ, and has given us the ministry of reconciliation; that is, in Christ God was reconciling the world to himself, not counting their trespasses against them, and entrusting the message of reconciliation to us. So we are ambassadors for Christ, since God is making his appeal through us; we entreat you on behalf of Christ, be reconciled to God. (2 Cor 5:17–20)

One thing to notice in this passage is the tension between the "already," the sense that God has already reconciled us through Christ, and the "not yet": now be reconciled to God. Paul does not see this tension as an internal contradiction. Reconciliation is a grace-filled action of God toward all humanity. But it is also a part of the ongoing ministry of Christians in relationship to themselves and others. Paul asserts that he and his colleagues have become ambassadors of God.

Ambassadors are those who not only represent their leader but who also have the authority to make decisions in the name of their leader. They become instruments of reconciliation on behalf of God. Paul considered his message so vitally important to the Corinthians because he had undergone a serious breach of relationship with them at one time (seen in the defensive tone of 2 Cor 11—13). He also urges married couples to try to reconcile differences if at all possible when conflicts arise (1 Cor 7:11). Paul's understanding of reconciliation is another aspect of his position of hope in the world. Disputes, disagreements, or breaches of trust are never so hopeless that reconciliation is impossible. Paul believed it had to be worked at, but because reconciliation has been achieved in Christ, it is also possible to concretize it in our own lives.

The teaching of the Deutero-Pauline letters regarding reconciliation is consistent with this perspective. Ephesians, in particular, uses the image of reconciliation to speak of the unity of the Gentiles and the Jews in Christ.

> For he is our peace; in his flesh he has made both groups into one and has broken down the dividing wall, that is, the hostility between us. He has abolished the law with its commandments and ordinances, that he might create in himself one new humanity in place of the two, thus making peace, and might reconcile both groups to God in one body through the cross, thus putting to death that hostility through it. (Eph 2:14–16, see vv. 11–18)

I think Paul's hope in the power of reconciliation provides potent encouragement to all Christians always to work hard at reconciliation in the face of conflict. It is an act of surrender to the power of God that can make something quite new out of our old human divisions.

SEVEN

PAUL'S LEGACY

97. Why is Paul so important to Christianity?

Paul is important to Christianity for both historical and theological reasons. Since Paul is the earliest witness of Christian faith in the NT, he holds obvious importance from an historical perspective. For example, the oldest accounts of the resurrection of Jesus (1 Cor 15:1–11) and the Last Supper (1 Cor 11:23–26) are found in Paul. The letters written to his churches, such as at Corinth, also provide some of the earliest evidence of how such faith communities were organized and functioned, at least insofar as scholars are able to reconstruct them. In addition, the nature of Paul's letters provides a good resource for studying early Christian literary forms. The use of letters for communication, instruction, correction, and the like gives us a window into the ordinary lives of real people whose struggles, now centuries removed from our time, nonetheless mirror some of our own modern concerns. Moreover, Paul's letters remain an important resource for studying ancient forms of rhetoric.

But he is important for more than just historical reasons. He is also the first recorded Christian "theologian." You note that I place the word "theologian" in quotation marks. As we have said, Paul is not systematic in his theology. He certainly did not set out to invent a totally logical and self-enclosed theological system. Yet his letters express such basic elements to Christian faith that no theological system thereafter could afford to ignore Paul.

Yet another theological reason that Paul remains important for Christianity is the history of interpretation. Paul's impact was very wide ranging. He greatly influenced early Church fathers, such as John Chrysostom, Augustine, Theodore of Mopsuestia, and Jerome. Later Christian thinkers also benefited from Paul's legacy. Paul had enormous influence on important thinkers like Martin Luther, Charles Wesley, and Karl Barth. The Protestant

Reformation, in general, was weaned on Pauline thought, albeit at times from skewed or exaggerated interpretations of it. Many biblical scholars through the ages have written lengthy commentaries on Paul's letters, and these all can contribute to our understanding of Paul's long-lasting impact on Christian thought. Perhaps the most obvious reason to acknowledge Paul's importance is the testimony of the NT itself. The probability that at least some of the letters attributed to him stem from the hands of later admirers or colleagues or disciples indicates that Paul's legacy was important even to the early church. The existence of at least some Deutero-Pauline letters indicates that he had followers who sought to preserve his lasting contributions to the Christian faith. They recognized that his ideas had potential for a more universal impact on the life of the church than Paul likely anticipated. Early Christians recognized that Paul's vision, expressed through his letters, went far beyond the communities he served. The fact that his letters were the earliest canonical collection in the NT lends credence to this idea. Paul's letters, even in his lifetime, were recognized to have a broader application that could shape the life of future communities as well as his own. Finally, there is aesthetic value to Paul's letters. They are often poetic and inspirational. There is also beauty in Paul's letters, and that alone might suffice for some to reflect on them at length.

98. At times Paul's teachings sound intolerant. Was he a fundamentalist?

I can understand your impression that Paul may seem very stern at times, but to apply the term "fundamentalist" to him is problematic. In the first place, the term itself is slippery. In common parlance it has come to mean someone who is rigid and inflexible, but that is not the derivation of the word. Rather, it means someone who tries to uphold fundamentals, truly essential beliefs, or foundational truths. Viewed from this perspective, Paul can be considered one who tried to focus on essentials and not allow incidentals to interfere with what he thought were the central elements of the Christian faith. But I would still avoid applying the term "fundamentalist" to him because of a possible confusion with certain modern tendencies.

A second issue is whether Paul was really intolerant. True, he defended his own apostleship with fervor and verbally attacked those he believed were harming the faith. But Paul also recognized that the Jewish law had to be adapted in light of the gospel of Jesus Christ. Rather than legalistically holding onto the law, Paul showed great flexibility in applying it to followers of Christ. The need to bend it significantly to accommodate the Gentiles was a major move for someone who came out of a staunch Jewish background and who was extremely zealous in it. Furthermore, many of his letters directly or indirectly show that Paul could be very tolerant of less than perfect responses to the gospel. For example, his willingness in certain circumstances to adapt the Lord's teaching regarding marriage and separation (1 Cor 7), or his practical pastoral advice on many different topics in the Corinthian correspondence, hardly reveal someone who is unadaptable.

Yet one aspect of your question rings true. Paul was a man of intense conviction. He had a firm faith, and he was not afraid to speak his mind clearly when he thought the essentials of Christianity were at stake. In this sense, Paul comes across strongly. He is insistent that the gospel cannot be compromised in ways that would dull its edges. To live in Christ Jesus, according to Paul, requires accepting all that comes with faith, including the cross. Paul does not believe Christians should forsake the essentials to follow an easier path. I would consider this stance to be one of firm faith, rather than stubborn inflexibility.

99. What influence do Paul's letters have on church teachings?

Paul's influence on Christianity has been enormous, and the church's understanding of many aspects of Christian faith are due to Paul's letters. One could say that Paul directly or indirectly influenced the articulation of many elements of Christianity: the cross and resurrection; the multiple aspects of the Christ-event; baptism and reconciliation; justification by faith; salvation and redemption; the Christian virtues of faith, hope, and love; the Eucharist; marriage; the church as the body of Christ; the Holy Spirit and the gifts of the Spirit; spirituality and prayer; ethics; the parousia and coming judgment, among many others. In fact, there seems to be very little that Paul left out of his letters.

Even on a practical level Paul's influence can be felt. For example, the Catholic Church's specific practice of allowing what is called "the Pauline privilege" is based upon Paul's leniency toward marital situations that were complex and difficult to resolve within the normal framework of Christian marriage (1 Cor 7; see question 87).

100. Do Protestants and Catholics interpret Paul differently?

Yes, there are still differences of interpretation in Paul between Protestants and Catholics, but then, there are sometimes differences of approach to other biblical materials as well. (Remember that there are differences of approach among Roman Catholic scholars themselves.) Nonetheless, I emphasize that there has been tremendous convergence in interpretation of Paul today as compared to prior generations. Paul should no longer be singled out as the area where the most disagreement on interpretation exists. The contemporary doctrine of justification, for instance, is an area where the one-time abyss between classical Catholic and Lutheran interpretations has been bridged. This is due in no small measure to a lot of hard work on the part of biblical exegetes for both Churches, and the support and direction they have received from their respective church leaders.

More important on the question of interpretation is that scholars now judge the results of research and opinions not so much from denominational perspectives, but from more objective, scientific criteria. This is not to say that scholars actually achieve pure objectivity. All scholars have their biases that they bring to their work; denominational biases certainly exist. But these are usually not allowed to be the determining factor in one's interpretation of the Bible. If at one time, Roman Catholics could be said to be lacking in major authoritative commentaries on Paul's letters, that could not be said today. Such commentaries do exist (e.g., Joseph Fitzmyer and Brendan Byrne on Romans), but they engage in conversation with their Protestant counterparts on equal scholarly terms. In my judgment, Protestants and Catholics both have much to learn from one another when it comes to Paul, and have been open to doing so in recent decades. This bodes well for all future interpretations of the Pauline letters.

101. How would you recommend that we interpret Paul today? Is he really that relevant to our modern lifestyle?

After many years of teaching and preaching in various contexts, I am convinced that Paul is as relevant today as he ever was. That is why I wrote this book. It is also why I continue to preach among Catholics the value of Paul's writings that are often a neglected source of inspiration and spiritual enrichment. I also believe that many of Paul's letters give us very practical wisdom that can be adapted, at the very least by way of analogy, to situations in our own day. One example that quickly comes to mind is the Corinthian correspondence. Many Churches today are experiencing lack of internal unity and the reality of factions in a way that has been a rather persistent embarrassment throughout Christian history. Paul's pastoral approach, in which he both encourages and reprimands his congregation at the same time, provides an excellent reflection on how to promote deeper, more lasting Christian unity. I am not saying that there is always a one-to-one correspondence between Paul's teaching and our contemporary situation. We must acknowledge that Paul's world was very different than our own. Nonetheless, much of what Paul writes about is descriptive of the human condition in every age. Much of his advice and teaching speaks out across the ages and can still call us to reexamine our lives carefully.

In one sense, my advice on interpreting Paul is no different than my advice on biblical interpretation in general. I emphasize several basic principles that are essential to any act of biblical interpretation. First and foremost is the necessity of always placing the readings in their context. For Pauline passages, that means acknowledging the specific context of the letter in which the passage occurs. Each letter has its own unique background that provides the appropriate context for interpreting specific passages. Additionally, each passage has its own context within the letter, providing clues for the careful interpreter. Context is always of importance.

A second piece of advice is to work your way gradually into the Pauline corpus. Do not begin with the Letter to the Romans. Begin rather with one of the more practical letters, like First Corinthians, First Thessalonians, or Philippians. Trying to tackle some of Paul's more profound or complex thoughts too early can bog one down quickly.

Third, remember to read the letters *as* letters. They were written to real flesh-and-blood members of beloved communities that Paul sought to advise pastorally. Placing ourselves in a similar position may help us listen to Paul's voice more authentically, even though we will not always understand every reference that he makes in his letters.

Finally, we should be mindful that as with so many other parts of scripture, not every passage corresponds to our contemporary situation in a one-to-one manner. Some of Paul's advice is based upon the culture of his day, such as the injunctions on hairstyles and coverings (1 Cor 11:3–16). These are not timeless ethical instructions but practical issues facing the community that Paul was addressing at the time. The vast majority of passages in

Paul, however, do have something to say to Christians of all time. That is why the best advice I can give is simply to pick up Paul's letters and read them for yourself. If you allow yourself the experience, you will find much in them both to nourish and challenge your own faith for years to come.

RECOMMENDATIONS FOR FURTHER READING

Because this list is intended primarily for a nontechnical audience, many classic and older references are excluded. Many of the books, however, contain further bibliographies that can lead the interested reader to helpful resources.

Richard S. Ascough, *What Are They Saying About the Formation of Pauline Churches?* New York/Mahwah, N.J.: Paulist Press, 1998. A good overview of how scholars assess the background of Paul's churches, including both Jewish and Hellenistic-Roman influences.

C. K. Barrett, *Paul: An Introduction to His Thought.* Louisville, Ky: Westminster/John Knox, 1994. A fine popular introduction to Paul and his letters by an important British scholar.

Vincent Branick, *House Church in the Writings of Paul.* Zacchaeus Studies. Collegeville, Minn.: The Liturgical Press, 1989. A basic introduction to the concept of the "house church" in the Pauline letters.

Raymond E. Brown, *An Introduction to the New Testament.* New York: Doubleday, 1997, esp. pp. 409–680. Embedded in this monumental NT Introduction are masterful summaries of Paul's letters and the scholarly issues surrounding them, all in a readable format.

Charles B. Cousar, *The Letters of Paul.* Interpreting Biblical Texts. Nashville, Tenn.: Abingdon, 1996. A good basic introduction to Paul and his letters, offering outlines of each Pauline letter and an explanation of theological themes.

James D. G. Dunn, *The Theology of Paul the Apostle.* Grand Rapids, Mich.: Eerdmans, 1998. Formidable and technical, but one of the most cogent contemporary presentations of Paul's theology, primarily focusing on Romans.

Joseph A. Fitzmyer, *Paul and His Theology: A Sketch.* Englewood Cliffs, N.J.: Prentice-Hall, 1989. Also available in the *New Jerome Biblical Commentary* (R. E. Brown et al., eds.). Englewood Cliffs, N.J.: Prentice-Hall, 1990, pp. 1382–1416. A succinct yet thorough summary of Paul and the main areas of his teaching, written by an important Roman Catholic interpreter.

Victor Paul Furnish, *Jesus According to Paul.* Understanding Jesus Today. Cambridge: Cambridge University Press, 1993. A brief but thorough presentation of how Paul's letters refer to Jesus and his teachings.

Florence Gillman, *Women Who Knew Paul.* Zacchaeus Studies. Collegeville, Minn.: The Liturgical Press, 1992. A brief but useful summary of a neglected area of study in the Pauline corpus; namely, Paul's female companions.

Michael J. Gorman, *Cruciformity: Paul's Narrative Spirituality of the Cross.* Grand Rapids, Mich.: Eerdmans, 2001. A more technical but readable presentation of Paul's theology, emphasizing the cross, faith, hope, love, and power.

Mark Harding, *What Are They Saying About the Pastoral Epistles?* New York/Mahwah, N.J.: Paulist Press, 2001. A helpful summary of scholars' positions about 1 and 2 Timothy and Titus, including the question of authorship.

Daniel J. Harrington, *Paul on the Mystery of Israel.* Zacchaeus Studies. Collegeville, Minn.: The Liturgical Press, 1992. A lucid explanation of the challenging chapters in Romans that address how Israel will eventually be saved by God's action (Rom 9—11).

Gerald D. Hawthorne, et al. (eds.), *Dictionary of Paul and His Letters*. Downers Grove, Ill.: InterVarsity, 1993. An essential reference tool that contains entries on more than two hundred topics about Paul and his letters, written from a scholarly evangelical Christian perspective.

David G. Horrell, *An Introduction to the Study of Paul.* New York/London: Continuum, 2000. A compact introduction to Paul and his letters organized topically, such as Paul's life, Paul as a letter-writer, Paul's theology, and so on.

Leander E. Keck, *Paul and His Letters,* 2nd ed. Philadelphia: Fortress, 1988. Though dated, this is a good, readable presentation of major theological themes in Paul's letters from an important Protestant scholar.

Veronica Koperski, *What Are They Saying About Paul and the Law?* New York/Mahwah, N.J.: Paulist Press, 2001. A good overview of how scholars approach the disputed topic of Paul's treatment of the law (torah).

Frank J. Matera, *Strategies for Preaching Paul.* Collegeville, Minn.: The Liturgical Press, 2001. Provides a fine introduction to the Pauline letters while addressing the practical question of how to preach from Paul's letters.

———, *New Testament Ethics: The Legacies of Jesus and Paul.* Louisville, Ky.: Westminster/John Knox, 1996, Part II, pp. 119–247. Technical but very readable presentation of Paul's ethical legacy, including the disputed letters.

Jerome Murphy-O'Connor, *Paul the Letter-Writer: His World, His Options, His Skills.* Collegeville, Minn.: The Liturgical Press, 1995. An interesting and informative assessment of Paul that provides a great deal of background on the practice of ancient letter-writing.

Charles B. Puskas, Jr., *The Letters of Paul: An Introduction.* Good News Studies #25. Collegeville, Minn.: The Liturgical Press, 1993. A thorough general introduction to Paul and his letters, useful as a textbook; also includes a chapter on the Letter to the Hebrews.

Calvin J. Roetzel, *Letters of Paul: Conversations in Context*, 4th ed. Louisville, Ky.: Westminster/John Knox, 1998. A standard textbook that provides a comprehensive but user-friendly introduction to Paul emphasizing the context of each Pauline letter.

————, *Paul: The Man and the Myth*. Minneapolis, Minn.: Fortress, 1999. An award-winning presentation of what can be known about Paul as a person.

J. Paul Sampley, *Walking Between the Times: Paul's Moral Reasoning*. Minneapolis, Minn.: Augsburg Fortress, 1991. A clear exposition of Paul's moral teaching written from the perspective of Paul's eschatology.

E. P. Sanders, *Paul*. Past Masters. Oxford: Oxford University Press, 1991. A short but incisive introduction to Paul and his thought from the scholar whose major, more technical work gave rise to the "new perspective" on Paul.

Anthony J. Tambasco, *In the Days of Paul: The Social World and Teaching of the Apostle*. New York/Mahwah, N.J.: Paulist Press, 1991. An informative and popular presentation of the social world behind Paul's letters.

Thomas Tobin, *The Spirituality of Paul*. Message of Biblical Spirituality #12. Wilmington, Del.: Michael Glazier, 1987. A popular presentation of the spiritual aspects of Paul's thought.

Wolfgang Trilling, *A Conversation with Paul*. New York: Crossroad, 1987. An older but popular treatment of Paul by a major German scholar.

David Wenham, *Paul: Follower of Jesus or Founder of Christianity?* Grand Rapids, Mich.: Eerdmans, 1995. An extensive, more technical assessment of the continuing controversy about Paul as the founder of Christianity.

————, *Paul and Jesus: The True Story*. Grand Rapids, Mich.: Eerdmans, 2002. A carefully argued book, if at times straining to prove a point, that tries to show how close Paul's teachings were to those of Jesus.

Ben Witherington, III, *The Paul Quest: The Renewed Search for the Jew of Tarsus.* Downers Grove, Ill.: InterVarsity, 1998. An astute study of data on the "historical Paul" by a prolific Protestant author; technical but very readable.

N. T. Wright, *What Saint Paul Really Said: Was Paul of Tarsus the Real Founder of Christianity?* Grand Rapids, Mich.: Eerdmans, 1997. An accessible presentation of how to interpret Paul that counters ongoing accusations that Paul distorted Jesus' teachings.

John Ziesler, *Pauline Christianity,* rev. ed. New York: Oxford University Press, 1990. A short, readable basic introduction to Paul's letters.

APPENDIX

MAPS OF PAUL'S MISSIONARY JOURNEYS
(Cf. Description in Question 30, pp. 59–63)

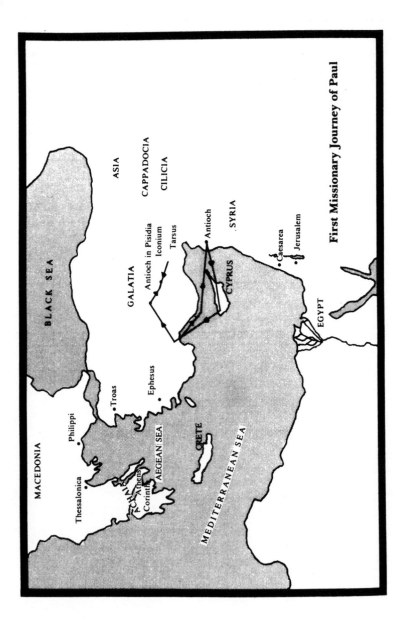

First Missionary Journey of Paul

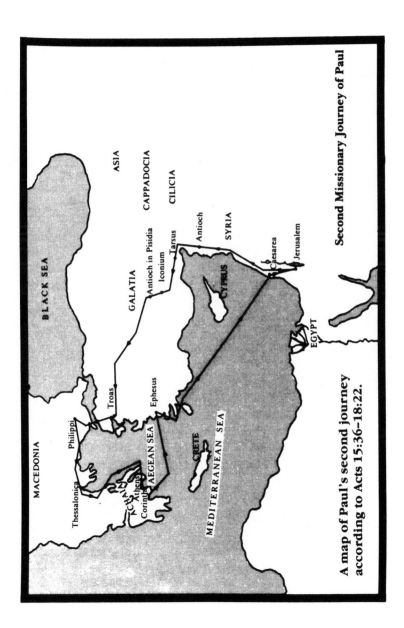

Second Missionary Journey of Paul

A map of Paul's second journey according to Acts 15:36–18:22.

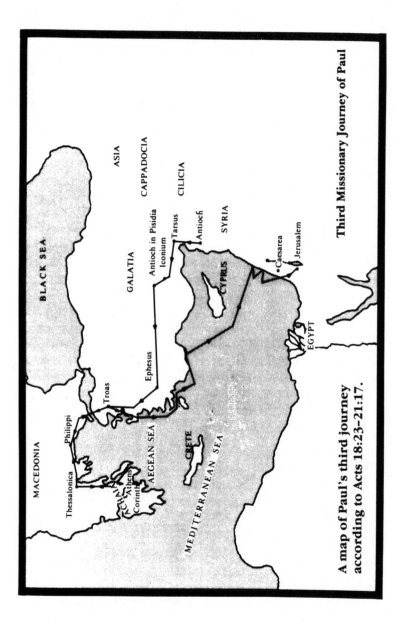

Third Missionary Journey of Paul

A map of Paul's third journey
according to Acts 18:23–21:17.

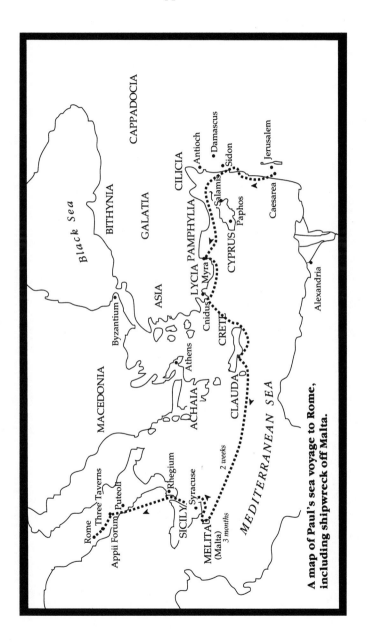

A map of Paul's sea voyage to Rome, including shipwreck off Malta.

RESPONSES TO 101 QUESTIONS ON ISLAM
by John Renard

RESPONSES TO 101 QUESTIONS ON HINDUISM
by John Renard

RESPONSES TO 101 QUESTIONS ON BUDDHISM
by John Renard

RESPONSES TO 101 QUESTIONS ON THE MASS
by Kevin W. Irwin

RESPONSES TO 101 QUESTIONS ON GOD AND EVOLUTION
by John F. Haught

RESPONSES TO 101 QUESTIONS ON
CATHOLIC SOCIAL TEACHING
by Kenneth R. Himes, O.F.M.